Ebbets Field

Brooklyn's Baseball Shrine

by

Joseph McCauley

© 2004 Joseph McCauley
All Rights Reserved.

No part of this book may be reproduced, stored in a retrieval system, or transmitted by any means without the written permission of the author.

First published by AuthorHouse 10/28/04

ISBN: 1-4184-8155-6 (sc)

Library of Congress Control Number: 2004097103

Printed in the United States of America
Bloomington, Indiana

This book is printed on acid-free paper.

authorHOUSE

1663 LIBERTY DRIVE
BLOOMINGTON, INDIANA 47403
(800) 839-8640
www.authorhouse.com

Ebbets Field Brooklyn's Baseball Shrine

Chapter 1	Charles Ebbets Dream Realized 1	
	(1913)	
Chapter 2	Uncle Robbie Arrives – Visionary Dies 6	
	(1914-1931)	
Chapter 3	Depression & Depressing Times 11	
	(1931-1937)	
Chapter 4	A Hard Drinking, Red headed Moses 15	
	(1938-1942)	
Chapter 5	War Years & the Rickey Revolution 21	
	(1942-1948)	
Chapter 6	Fans in the Stands 29	
Chapter 7	More Than a Ballpark 38	
	(other events at Ebbets Field)	
Chapter 8	Wait Till Next Year - Winning and Heartbreaks 46	
	(1948-1954)	
Chapter 9	Favorite Dodger Players 54	
Chapter 10	Workers at Ebbets Field 61	
Chapter 11	Players Remember Ebbets Field 69	
Chapter 12	Hot Dog Stories 73	
Chapter 13	This Is Next Year 76	
	(1955)	
Chapter 14	The Last Years 80	
	(1956-1957)	
Chapter 15	Fans and Ballpark Abandoned 86	

Chapter 1   Charles Ebbets Dream Realized

Welcome to Ebbets Field.

There's an eggshell blue sky and fifty one degrees outside on April 5, 1913 and no keys are available to open the bleachers, no flag is there to run up the flagpole and no press box has been built in Brooklyn's new $750,000 steel and concrete baseball palace. Outside the stadium, cars, trolley cars and horse drawn carriages bring fans past hot dog vendors into a modern marvel on Sullivan Street and Cedar Place. Fans stream through the main entrance and see an ornate rotunda, an 80 foot circle enclosed in Italian marble, as they dodge the esthetic and fragrant floral pieces placed there.

The floor is tiled with what looks like stitches of a baseball and overhead is a chandelier with 12 baseball bat arms holding a dozen baseball shaped globes hanging from the 27 ft. high stucco ceiling that is decorated with stars and clouds. Each woman receives a souvenir hand mirror as she enters the gates while Mr. Tom Shannon's band plays excerpts from "The Rose Maid" and "Jolly Fellows". There are also 12 turnstiles and an equal number of golden ticket windows to handle the overflow crowd compared to the four at old Washington Park. An aide scurries to find the keys and a flag is found as a capacity crowd of 24,000 fans (10,000 are turned away) jam inside to watch Casey Stengel hit a fifth inning inside –the -park home run to lead the Superbas to a 3-2 victory over the cross town rival New York Yankees in an exhibition game.

At least 7,000 fans watch from the bluffs above the field at Montgomery Street and Bedford Avenue and they let out thunderous applause after Jake Daubert's 6th inning home run.

So begins an unusual, strange and often entertaining 47 years of baseball and other events at Ebbets Field, in the borough that was once a city. Four days later, the inaugural opening day game was played before 14,000 freezing fans on a rainy and windy Wednesday. Shannon's Twenty-Third Regiment band played while Mrs. Ed McKeever (wife of the vice- president of the club) raised the flag and ballplayers from both teams gathered about her. Owner Charles Ebbets himself sang the national anthem. All five borough representatives were there as Brooklyn Borough President Alfred Steers threw out the first ball.

There was no grass yet in the outfield (until July) but other than that most were satisfied with the new park that had such architectural details as pilasters and ornate capitals on the outside and was "fireproof". Unfortunately, the home team lost a pitcher's duel to Philadelphia 1-0 but fans took pride in their team's new home. Charles Hercules Ebbets had seen his dream come true.

Ebbets worked his way up through the Brooklyn ball club in Horatio Alger fashion by selling tickets, score cards and performing other mundane chores.

He had previously been in the publishing business and had even sold books door-to-door when his salesmen couldn't dispose of their stock. George Chauncey, one of the four "kings" owners of the Brooklyn team, took a liking to Ebbets and offered him stock in the club just as it joined the National League in 1890. The team had previously spent six years in the American Association. Ebbets actually managed the team in 1898 and finished in tenth place with a 38-68 record. After that season, Ebbets took Chaucey up on his offer. The Brooklyn squad had been known as the Trolley Dodgers in honor of the Brooklyn faithful who avoided injury by scurrying out of the way of careening public transportation as they attempted to cross streets. Many actually were hit by the trolley cars while walking to the park. In 1889, they were renamed the Bridegrooms because six of the players had gotten married during the season.

Within seven years, Charlie Ebbets had consolidated his position in the club. In 1896, one of the owners and secretary (Joseph Doyle) died and Ebbets succeeded him. The next year, another owner passed away (Charles Bryne) and Ebbets was elected president of the team, now called Dodgers.

Ebbets moved the team from their home in East New York to a spot between First and Third and Third and Fourth Avenue and called the field Washington Park. George Washington had fought a battle on the spot and it was named after him. By 1899, the Dodgers became known as the Superbas because the manager's name was the same as Hanlon of the Superbas vaudeville troupe. Ned Hanlon led Brooklyn to their first pennant in 1890.

Meanwhile, Ebbets had to deal with Harry Von der Horst, owner of the Baltimore Orioles. Von der Horst incredibly was able to buy controlling interest of the Dodgers while Ebbets picked up a few more shares and retained his title. At the turn of the century, the Superbas once again won the pennant but storm clouds, from the upstart American League, hovered over the franchise. Player raids from the new league and sagging attendance convinced co-owner Ferdinand Abell to sell his stock to Ebbets in 1902.

C. Ebbets (center) at opening day

When Von der Horst was ready to throw in the towel, Ebbets was in a financial bind. Manager Hanlon decided he would like to buy the club and move it back to Baltimore (where he had success earlier in his career by winning two pennants). With the threat of the team moving and his job leaving with them, Ebbets borrowed money from a Brooklyn furniture dealer friend, Henry Medicus and bought controlling interest in the team.

Charles Ebbets had come full circle from a lowly gofer to owner of his hometown Brooklyn Dodgers. Remarkably, after several mediocre seasons and several manager changes, Ebbets was still able to make money by keeping expenses low. In 1908, seating capacity was too small at Washington Park and after considering expanding it, Ebbets rejected the idea and began looking at other sites. He began to check out the location of trolley lines and cost of land in an underdeveloped area of Flatbush. Ebbets then set up a dummy company and started buying 40 parcels of land in Pigtown where farmers used to come and feed their pigs.

In 1912, he had purchased the site (just east of Prospect Park) for $100,000 and announced his intention to build a new, fireproof park there. Some people thought he was crazy but Ebbets had envisioned the borough growing and expanding outward to his location and he was right. An incident on opening day of 1912 proved that a new park was a necessity when a near riot broke out when the Superbas hosted the defending champion (and hated rivals) New York Giants. "The game wasn't scheduled to start until 4pm, but there was so large a crowd about the park at noon that the gates were opened then," according to Frank Graham in his book "Brooklyn Dodgers".

"By 1:30 the stands were packed, and by 2:30 the congestion was so great the Fire Department ordered that no more be admitted. But when the attendants closed the gates, the fans went over and

Opening day at Ebbets Field 1913

under the fences, surged down through the stands and packed themselves so closely on the field that when play began, the players had no room in which to run for foul flies. Minor fights, precipitated by the crowding and jostling broke out in the stands. In the press box, reporters screamed at fans standing in front to sit down or move, so they might see the ball game," Graham noted.

The Police Commissioner Bingham refused to send police to use force inside Washington Park but once Mayor William J. Gaynor heard about the disorder "he ordered the cops inside". With the Giants leading 18 to 3, Umpire Bill Klem called the game because of darkness in the sixth inning thus saving life, limb and keeping the stands from being wrecked.

After new parks were built in Boston and Detroit, Ebbets saw the need to move out of his antiquated, wooden firetrap into a larger and more modern home for his team. However, Ebbets hit a snag in building his new baseball park…lack of money. He solved this by selling half interest in the club in August to the McKeever brothers (Ed and Steve) who were contractors for $100.000.

When it came time to name the park, Ebbets was going to name it Washington Park but sports writers convinced him to name it after himself since they said "You paid for it". One year after the Titanic sank and just before the world's tallest building (The Woolworth Building) was unveiled across the Brooklyn Bridge in Manhattan, Charles Ebbets had his new palace.

Ebbets wrote in Leslie's Weekly that his park "will contain every convenience that we can

No press box, 1920

devise and will be absolutely safe. I will no longer have to worry about fires, collapsing stands and other dangers that menace the spectators and of which they seldom give thought".

There was 1,700 tons of steel used in the grandstand, 40,000 feet of gas pipe and 250,000 feet of wire used for construction of pipe railing at Ebbets Field. The total length of the main grandstand at the back of the first deck was 807 ft 6 inches, the field stand was 155ft 6in, making the total length of stand constructed 963 feet. The roof was 80 feet above the playing field and at the corner of Sullivan and Bedford Ave. it was 100ft above the curb (or the height of a ten-story apartment house). In constructing the cornices and ornamental railings, there were furnished 900 feet of galvanized iron main cornice at roof level 5 feet 6 inches high, 60 baseball finials and 900 feet of galvanized iron cornice and gutter lining at eave of tile roof. The original dimensions of the park were… right field - 295 ft from home plate, left field - 401 ft and center field about 425 ft (depending on the angle). Initially, with the exception of right field, Ebbets Field was a pitcher's park.

Pig Town site of Ebbets Field

The reinforced concrete assured the stands were fireproof and unlikely to collapse. Ebbets had seen the Polo Grounds in Manhattan burn to the ground (as had several other parks) and wanted a safe environment for fans and his investment. After Ebbets graduated from public schools, he took up architecture with the firm of William T. Beer and drew up the working plans for the Metropolitan Hotel and Niblo's Gardens. This experience helped him with the construction of Ebbets Field. However, not every thing went smoothly in the construction process. Strange things happened at Ebbets Field even before it opened. To help fertilize the ground, the McKeever brothers imported fish "chum" from their factory at Egg Harbor. This did not make them popular in the surrounding areas because the "chum" had the "most aggressive odor known to science" according to the Brooklyn Daily Eagle.

Ebbets Field under construction

Professional Gardener Mike Daly who prepared the field for opening day noticed that one of the Castle brothers (who had a contract to fill the park) bought the wrong dirt to fill in the outfield. Evidently, one of the brothers saw an impressive load of rich, black dirt in a wagon on the street and figured it would be perfect for Ebbets Field. After paying $2 a load, seventy loads were laid on Ebbets

Field. When Daly examined it, he was furious and made a beeline to see Charlie Ebbets. Daly explained to Ebbets that the soil might be good for some uses but not for his field. He said it would "hold water like a sponge and a Christmas shower would not dry out before Columbus Day" according to the Eagle. Ebbets agreed to have it removed and he had to pay the wagoners $2 a load to dig up and carry away the seventy loads that had been put down. Although Daly had the infield sodded and in perfect shape, the outfield remained barren until mid summer because of this fiasco. The highlight of the 1913 season was the MVP performance of first baseman Jake Daubert. His batting average of .350 led the league but couldn't raise the Superbas any higher than 6th place in the standings. The next year 1914 saw the arrival of Wilbert Robinson who was to become a household name in Brooklyn.

Ebbets Field

Chapter 2   Uncle Robbie Arrives – Visionary Dies

Initially, Wilbert Robinson was hired in 1914 to be a coach but after Detroit refused overtures for Hughie Jennings services the managerial reins were turned over to the man fans eventually dubbed Uncle Robbie.

Robbie had a reputation of being a good handler of pitchers. Years previously, he was a catcher in Baltimore and a teammate of John McGraw's. He also held a major league record of seven straight hits in a nine inning game.

The late Harold Seymour in his Baseball-The Golden Age saw Robinson close up. "I well remember Robinson from the summer I spent on the bench with him as the Brooklyn batboy. He was bumbling, very profane and very fat. Though outwardly gruff, he was generally popular with Brooklyn fans and players. He was childishly superstitious. And when things went wrong, as they often did, he blamed various jinxes." "When the team was in a losing streak, he would grumble, 'We can't win in this goddam park'.

Robbie's warmth and simplicity made the fans feel that they had a personal share in the fortunes of the team and in helping him run it.

"He was always ready to argue strategy with them under the stands or in the street, and he accepted taunts as personal challenges. More than once I saw him step in front of the dugout to shout back at some particularly loud-mouthed heckler," said Seymour.

Wilbert Robinson

Mrs. Robinson accompanied her husband often to Ebbets Field and she became known to the fans as "Ma" Robinson with her husband affectionately called "Uncle Robbie". Under Robinson, two pennants flew over Ebbets Field's diamond in five years. In 1916, tobacco chewing Robbie witnessed his team lose to the Boston Red Sox four games to one in the World Series.

Republican candidate for President, Charles Evan Hughes attended the first game that the overwhelming favorite Red Sox won 6-5 at Braves Field.

Babe Ruth tossed a 6 hitter in winning the second game that lasted a record 14 innings. The Dodgers Sherrod Smith and Ruth became the first two left handers to start a World Series together in front of largest World Series crowd of 40,000 spectators.

Game three was overshadowed by German submarine attacks off Nantucket that forced President Woodrow Wilson to cancel attending Ebbets Field. Brooklyn won 4-3 and hundreds of fans threw seat cushions and hats into the air after the game and paraded around the park following the band that played there.

Game four sobered the Dodger faithful as Boston won 4-3 amid reports that Coney Island restaurant proprietor and businessman Charles Felt had offered to buy the team. Co-owner Ed McKeever said it would take $2 million to purchase the club.

Game five had the Sox close out the series at home in front of a new record crowd of 42,600. The 4-1 victory was Boston's forth title. Former owner of Boston's National League club, James Gaffney, also offered to buy the Dodgers during the series but was turned down.

Attendance that year reached 447,000 for the first time. It was 150,000 more than the previous year.

Within four years, Brooklyn had another pennant winner and 808,000 fans jammed inside Ebbets Field. The pitching staff included Leon Cadore who pitched the longest game in major league history that year. Cadore dueled Boston Braves Joe Oeschger on May 1 for the whole 26 innings in a 1-1 tie. The game was called because of darkness.

The 1920 series started out at Ebbets Field and it was a cold and blustery Tuesday Oct. 5 when the Dodgers took the field sporting new cream colored uniforms with dark pinstripes. Temporary bleachers were set up in deep right center field to accommodate an over flow crowd. Before the first game, many fans waited overnight in the rain to purchase unreserved seats. A Grand Jury was also resuming in Chicago at the same time to investigate the "fixing" of the 1919 World Series. The Dodgers and Indians were both cleared of any scandal before the game began.

Home Plate meeting before 1916 World Series

Charles Ebbets eliminated the presence of a brass band so that any available seats in the park would be given to fans. Demand for tickets was so great scalpers were selling $1.10 pavilion seats for $12. First game attendance was 28,804 in the 25,000 seat park. Writers in the press box were each treated to a half pint of rye, courtesy of Charlie Ebbets, even though prohibition was on.

The next day, federal agents raided Ebbets Field after a writer hinted at the hospitality in a story. The press box was searched and even Ebbets private office was ransacked but the Feds came up empty. Charlie had been tipped off and the hooch had been removed. The series was tied at two games each when bad karma struck the Brooklyn squad with the only unassisted triple play in series history. With men on first and second base in the fifth inning, batter Clarence Mitchell smashed a liner to the right of second base. Cleveland's second sacker Bill Wambsganss stabbed the liner with one hand for the first out, stepped on second base for a force out and tagged Otto Miller (the runner approaching from first base) for the third out. Brooklyn never recovered and lost the series five games to two. Robinson's laissez-faire style of managing and the club's growing lack of talent finally caught up with them and they became known as the "daffiness boys" as the twenties and early thirties rolled along. Uncle Robbie didn't help matters after instituting a "bonehead club" for players screwing up, he became its first member when he turned in an incorrect lineup card at home plate before a game.

"Although he usually had a few good pitchers like Dazzy Vance and Jesse Petty and a first rate hitter, Babe Herman, Robbie had his hands full trying to put together a winning team," Harold Seymour said.

Herman typified the brand of ball played then. He was often the leader in hitting but his outfield play was atrocious and his base running even worse. He once doubled into a double play and ended up on third base with two other teammates. In spite of that, he had knocked in the winning run on that play. In another game, after smashing a liner off the wall in right field, Herman ran past the runner ahead of him while admiring his achievement. Herman was one of the original "good hit-no field" type of player who resented his tag as being kind of goofy. He let a reporter know of his displeasure one day in an interview and a writer was about to leave with a better appreciation of him when Herman pulled a lit cigar out of his pant's pocket and took a puff.

Temporary bleachers for 1920 World Series

It was during this time that a writer noticed a fan, that sat behind home plate and yelled, "You bum you" and "Youse Bums Youse" when the whole team disgusted him. A local writer noticed and soon the team's nickname became "The Bums".

Unfortunately, all Robbie had to work with were has beens and journeymen ballplayers. As a result, the team never won another pennant under him. While Robinson was handling the players, Ebbets was becoming the dean of baseball owners.

Charles Ebbets was also a visionary in baseball.

His often quoted line at the turn of the century about baseball "being in its infancy" was true. He pioneered many changes and practices to help it grow up. Among them were stopping the player parades from their hotel to the ballpark and back in horse drawn carriages. According to noted baseball historian Harold Seymour, these parades "subjected visiting players to the jeers and missiles of fans" along the route, as well as traveling in sweaty uniforms after the game. Ebbets even got the National League to install showers with hot and cold water and lockers for visiting teams in 1906. It took a while for full compliance but by 1909, all carriage parades were banned. Ebbets promoted his team by advertising on trolley cars and elevated trains and he also gave away photos of team players to saloons. Another change came in rearranging the pre game helter-skelter team warm ups. In 1906, Ebbets suggested that each team take turns on the field with batting and fielding practice instead of all at once, which at times resulted in chaos and possible harm to fans and players. This ritual of each team having individual warm ups continues to this day

Hot dog vendors at 1920 World Series

Other ideas Ebbets came up with included special days for certain players, the rain check, the player option, putting numbers on players sleeves or hats, playing Sunday baseball and valet parking service for car owners. He also suggested the player draft, wherein last place teams would get first pick and first place teams last pick, of new ballplayers each year. As a member of the National League Schedule committee, he extended the season to include the new holiday of Columbus Day (October 10) For this, he earned the nickname of "Holiday Charlie".

Another innovation that backfired was trying out a public address system that was amplified. According to Tom Meany in the Story of the Brooklyn Dodgers, "the announcements were to be made by the umpire, who was wired for sound, believe it or not."

Fans in line for 1920 World series tickets

At first, nothing was heard but a crackling sound then (to the chagrin of most everyone in attendance) during a fifth inning rhubarb the umpire's abusive language toward a player came over loud and clear for all to hear. Charles Ebbets cancelled the experiment and it wasn't until 1936 that a P. A. system was installed at Ebbets Field.

The very year Ebbets Field was opened, Ebbets faced heavy competition from an upstart Federal League entry into Brooklyn at old Washington Park. World War I came on shortly thereafter and almost caused him financial ruin.

In 1915, Ebbets was offered $600,000 for his club. His partners (the McKeever brothers) were in favor of selling but Ebbets stubbornly refused to let go of his team. Because of ill health in May 1923 (he didn't attend opening day because of pneumonia), Ebbets was about to sell his half interest in the Dodgers but by August other club owners begged him not to retire. The rumor of New York Giants owner Charles Stoneham sale of his team to promoter Tex Richard and the Ringlings caused a panic among the other owners. They needed Ebbets to stabilize their situation.

Meanwhile, Charles Ebbets Jr. resigned after differences with co-owner Stephen McKeever. The senior Ebbets stayed on in spite of his doctor's wishes that he reside in Florida because of his asthma and heart problems.

By 1924, Ebbets saw his club achieve a profit of close to $500,000. Average attendance had jumped from 7,186 in 1923 to 10,645 in 1924. Total attendance was at 818,883 and that was a 254,000 jump in one season!

One reason for the jump was the Dodgers finished a season long struggle 1 and ½ games behind their arch rival New York Giants with a 92-62 record. At one point in late August, the Dodgers won fifteen straight games. They also won four straight doubleheaders!

During one game against the Giants, an over capacity crowd flowed through the rotunda and jumped over grandstand walls. They also used a telephone pole to ram through the center field gate to gain entrance. Another group of Dodger faithful smashed through the clubhouse window and ran over team trainer Doc Hart before they were held at bay by a policeman with a drawn revolver. Although the park's capacity was 25,000, there were 32,000 paying customers that day.

Even Commissioner Landis couldn't get into Ebbets Field until the seventh inning.

Ebbets had the mob roped off and twelve ground rule doubles were recorded. With that kind of fan allegiance, things never seemed brighter.

Unfortunately, during the spring training of 1925, Ebbets became ill and returned to the Waldorf-Astoria in New York where he died of heart disease on April 18 (opening day). After much consultation, it was decided to play the game with the hated Giants because, "Charlie wouldn't want anyone to miss the game just because he died," according to manager Wilbert Robinson. Crass as it sounds, Robinson was probably right. While the game was played, Ebbets hearse (with his body) passed by on its way to his home in Flatbush.

The National League did suspend the schedule on the day of his funeral two days later.

The hearse drove Ebbets body around the outfield of Ebbets Field as well as Washington Park before the funeral at Holy Trinity Episcopal Church.

While attending the Ebbets funeral, Acting President Ed McKeever caught pneumonia in a cold and pouring rain and died within a week. The front office of the Dodgers was in turmoil.

After some debate, Robinson became president with votes from Ebbet's heirs and briefly gave his position as manager to star player Zack Wheat. The team floundered and after six weeks, Robbie came back to right the ship but it was no use as the Dodgers sank with a 69-85 record into second division.

Making matters worse, Robinson and co-owner Steve McKeever were the baseball equivalent of the Bickersons (a 1940's radio comedy couple who constantly fought). Instead of being funny, kissing and making up, Robinson and McKeever hurled insults and after awhile stopped talking to each other.

Dodger star Zack Wheat with Robbie

Eventually, Robinson was president in title only and he saw his power wane and the team sank lower in the standings, as the years went on.

While the team was sliding, attendance was steady and Ebbets Field saw its first expansion one year after its founder passed away. Wooden bleachers were added in left field in the 1926 season. Previously, there hadn't been any seating in the outfield except on rare occasions when standing room was allowed.

John Crawford Nichols remembers that period,"I first went to Ebbets Field about the year 1926 when I was five. My dad was a big fan."

"There were wooden seats in left field (steel was erected about 1931). I think first capacity was 23,000 and later with a doubleheader with the 'Jints' they could crowd in over 36,000 if the fire department got free tickets," he chuckled.

The Robins (team name during Robbie's rein) struggled for the next few years and it wasn't until 1930 that they were in a pennant race. They actually led the league for a few weeks but finally finished in fourth place. Brooklyn fans, dubbed "The Flock," averaged over 14,000 per game for the first time. This was also the first year that attendance topped one million. With this in mind, another expansion of Ebbets Field began to take place.

Steel and concrete stands were being erected in left field and stretched over to center field. The scoreboard was also added in right field. However, in 1931, the Depression struck with a vengeance and attendance was down at Ebbets Field by 344,000 fans. The Robins finished with a disappointing 79-73 record. People were out of work in working class Brooklyn and stands were empty. It was becoming obvious Uncle Robbie's 18 year reign was coming to an end.

Chapter 3   Depression & Depressing Times

Charles Dillon Stengel (Casey)

When Wilbert Robinson's contract was not renewed after the 1931 season, Steve McKeever and the rest of the board decided to entrust the team to Max Carey. Carey had turned to baseball after his money ran out trying to pursue his dream of becoming a Lutheran Divinity minister. After being a star player on the Pittsburgh Pirates for many years, Carey finished his career with the Robins. It was hoped his disciplined style would make his former teammates see the light and be resurrected as a contending team in 1932.

Meanwhile, fan favorite and top hitter, Babe Herman was a spring training holdout. He had and off year and was given a cut in salary. He balked and was stunned when he was shipped out to Cincinnati in a trade with Carey's approval. Carey brought back Casey Stengel to Brooklyn from Toledo to coach. Times were tough as Casey was paid $7000 to coach (or $1500 less than he made as a minor league manager). The lure of Ebbets Field and the majors plus shrewd investments back home, enabled Casey's return to his baseball roots.

Second baseman Fresco Thompson, who played for Robinson and Carey, also noted Ebbets Field had a special charm in his book Every Diamond Doesn't Sparkle. "Ebbets Field had an intimacy found in no other ball park. Playing the infield you experienced the same feelings you'd have if you were entertaining thousands of unruly people in the sitting room of your home. If a fan whispered, it traveled nearly to second base and what reached your ears wasn't exactly music if someone called you a bum. One day at second base, I heard a fan discussing his wife's infidelities," Thompson said. Thompson, like Herman, didn't make it out of spring training either. He was optioned out to Jersey City after a personality clash with Carey. Carey's main acquisition in 1932 was former colossus Hack Wilson who knocked in 190 runs two years before (a record that still stands today). Wilson contributed a respectable .297 average with 23 homeruns and 123 runs batted in but he was out of the majors in two years after hitting the bottle harder than a baseball. Lefty O'Doul was the bright spot in 1932 as he led the Dodgers and the National League in batting with a .368 average but the team finished in third place.

That season, wooden bleachers in left field were replaced with steel and concrete bleachers. With people asking "Brother can you spare a dime," many of those seats remained empty most of the time any way. A formal press box had been installed in 1929 under the upper deck behind home plate. The original press box was in the first rows of the upper deck (after none had been built when Ebbets Field first opened). Unfortunately, there wasn't much to write home about in the next few years.

Owner Steve McKeever (now 78 years old), who had an offer for the team in 1929 from a group led by New York Mayor Jimmy Walker, must have wondered why he didn't sell out after witnessing attendance plummet over 50% from 1930 to 1933, With the team struggling on the field in 1933, rumors of Carey's imminent departure grew but McKeever smoothed that over in August by giving him a new contract for 1934. The Dodgers finished in 6th place and the red ink was mounting.

Several front office personal were shuffled around and others abandoned ship. In a scene that is reminiscent of the Abbott and Costello comedy routine "Who's on first," Casey Stengel was summoned from his home in California in late February and offered Carey's job. Naturally, Casey inquired about his friend,"What about Carey. Does he know yet?"

Bedford Avenue view 1936

No one had gotten around to telling Max Carey that he had been fired. Stengel waited until Carey was notified by phone that his services were no longer required (but his contract would be honored) before accepting the manager's position.

Baseball writers were amused that while the Dodgers were bleeding red ink, they could afford to pay two managers at the same time. Carey, naturally upset, wondered how they could expect him "to win the pennant during the off season". He also complained about front office interference during his whole stint as manager. Stengel arrived as a popular ex Dodger and coach under Carey. John Crawford Nichols, a loyal Dodger fan, recalls seeing him in 1934. "One day while trying to get autographs, I saw Casey Stengel and his wife come out of the rotunda and he stopped and showed us a bandage on his writing finger. He said he was sorry he could not sign for us. After he got in the cab, he turned and out of the back window, Stengel laughed and took off the false bandage," Nichols said. "That was better than getting him to sign. He was a funny man, fine player and a good manager," Nichols added.

Ray Berres, an ex-Dodger who is now in his mid 90's, also recalls Stengel fondly. "I only spent two years in Brooklyn and they were very enjoyable years. There was something going on at all times. The fans were great, fun loving people and rarely booed. Stengel was the manager and he added to the excitement." Berres said. About the only excitement for the sixth place Dodgers in 1934 occurred on the last two days of the season. Behind the Giants and Cardinals by twenty games, the Dodgers had a chance to pay back New York manager Bill Terry for his preseason slight of Brooklyn's finest.

Sizing up his team's prospects for the coming season, Terry had mentioned rivals except the Dodgers. When a reporter pointed out their absence in his critique, Terry joked "Is Brooklyn still in the league?"

Many Brooklyn fans visited Harlem's Polo Grounds for the final season series to see the Dodgers knock off the hated Giants and ruin their pennant hopes. Dodger's fan swamped the field and celebrated as if they had won a pennant. Casey was rewarded with a contract for three more years. Dodger player Jimmy Bucher enjoyed playing for Stengel. "Casey was one of the most compassionate and humane managers I ever played for. He always helped his players every way he could, off the field as well as on. His (Casey's) advice was worth following. I know! Once in St. Louis he advised us to get a good night's sleep. I didn't…I went out on the town…and when I got in late I ran into Casey. All he said was, 'Hi ya Kid'," Bucher said in his memoir A Baseball Life. "The next afternoon, with the temperature above 100, he left me in two full games of a doubleheader while everyone else got off with no more than five innings.

Every time Casey passed me on the field, he'd say, 'How ya doin' kid'? If Casey had fined me, it would have hurt. But the penalty I got helped me through many years of baseball," Bucher said.

The next two years, saw the Dodgers average only about 6,000 people per game. Harry Eisenstat pitched two seasons for Casey and he noted "They didn't draw as much because that was during the depression years. However, "the fans really made you want to play there". According to Eisenstat, "they carried on quite a bit and it was a good ball park to play in".

Stengel did his best to distract fans and writers from the terrible product on the field. He protested a game being played in the rain by using an umbrella in the coaching box. Another time, he offered an umpire a flashlight as darkness overwhelmed the ballpark in a game the Dodgers were winning.

At the end of the 1936 season, Casey was walking the plank even though he too had a year to go on his contract. Baseball writers held a going away party for Casey and lambasted the organization in their columns.

Burleigh Grimes (old Stubblebeard) was brought in to fire up the troops and battle the opponents in 1937. Grimes had pitched 19 years in the majors and had a 23-11 record on the 1920 pennant winning Robins. Grimes had his famous temper on display often that year. After constantly arguing with umpires and becoming a fan favorite, Grimes' Dodgers finished in 6th place with a 62-91 mark, 33 ½ games out of first. Not exactly the results the board was looking for especially when box seats were being added in center field during the winter of 1937 and 1938 at Ebbets Field.

However, three deals completed by the generally competent General Manager John Gorman (Dec. 1936 to Oct. 1937) would pay dividends years later. Cookie Lavagetto, Freddie Fitzsimmons and a good fielding, light hitting shortstop named Leo Durocher joined the Dodgers. "I'll never forget Cookie Lavagetto," Dodger fan John Nichols said. "As a kid, when he was a 19 year old rookie second baseman for the Pirates, a few of us kids chased him up Franklin Avenue towards Eastern Parkway. "A player taking the subway," we thought? "Finally, he stopped and was wonderful to us," Nichols said.

Meanwhile, Ebbets Field was beginning to resemble the mess on the field. Broken seats numbering in the thousands weren't repaired, paint was peeling throughout the park, and thugs (disguised as ushers) were as likely to strong arm customers as to show them to their seats.

In 1937, the team's business offices at 215 Montague Street had the telephones regularly turned off from nonpayment and the waiting room was usually filled with bill collectors and process servers. The

McKeever & Beford Ave

Brooklyn Trust Company was owed $500,000 but didn't foreclose because it also held the mortgage to Ebbets Field. Other owners were concerned that the Dodgers hadn't made a profit since 1930.

Finally, heirs of Ebbets and McKeever plus the Brooklyn Trust Company decided to consult National League President Ford Frick in finding a man to resurrect the dying franchise. They needed a man to lead them out of the wilderness. Branch Rickey was their first choice but he suggested a protégé of his …Larry MacPhail.

Chapter 4   A Hard Drinking, Red headed Moses

Leland Stanford (Larry) MacPhail was part Barnum and Bailey huckster, creative genius and sometime alcohol-fueled Tasmanian devil who was born in Cass City, Michigan to a prosperous banking family.

At 48, MacPhail had an impressive resume that included being a scholar, lawyer, banker, athlete, merchant, soldier and baseball entrepreneur. He was on leave from baseball in 1937 because he feared he was having a nervous breakdown after tangling with owner, radio magnet Powell Crosley Jr. Of course, his slugging a police sergeant in a hotel lobby didn't help either.

In the early 30's, MacPhail had successfully run the Columbus franchise in the American Association (where he first encountered Branch Rickey). Columbus had a working relationship with Rickey's St Louis Cardinals of the National League and MacPhail convinced them to install lights in the Ohio park. He parted ways with Columbus when his desire for a winning team clashed with the Cardinals desire to develop players for the big league club.

MacPhail moved on the Cincinnati where a local bank had control over the Reds. He convinced local radio pioneer Powell Crosley Jr. to option the team and install lights for night games.

The Reds played the major league's first night game on May 24, 1935 after President Franklin Roosevelt threw the switch at the White House to turn on the lights. MacPhail also hired an unknown southerner Red Barber, to broadcast radio games. He convinced Powell that radio was a perfect way to sell his team and make money along the way.

The raspy voiced, red haired MacPhail built up the Reds farm system and they were becoming a formidable opponent when he departed the scene (after some said he actually punched out Powell in an argument) in 1936.

The Reds won the National League pennants in 1939 and 1940 but Larry had moved onto his next challenge …the languishing Brooklyn Dodgers.

MacPhail met George McLaughlin and the rest of the Brooklyn board of directors and told them he wanted total control of the club if he was to turn it around. When they at first hesitated, he threatened to leave and they quickly capitulated. He got a three year contract and became executive vice president with complete authority to run the team. One of his first things he did was borrow $200,000 to fix up Ebbets Field (box seats were added in center field during the winter of 1937-38) and another $75,000 to purchase Philadelphia Phillies holdout Dolph Camilli. First baseman Camilli was a left handed slugger who could take advantage of Ebbets Field short right field wall. Shortly after Camilli arrived, club president Steve McKeever caught pneumonia and died at the age of 83.

Cedar Place outside of Ebbets Field was renamed McKeever Place in time for opening day of 1938. McKeever who got along with everyone (except Wilbert Robinson) had promised "I'll hold my share as long as I live, and my family will carry on after that," held true to his word and never gave up his ownership. His stock in the team passed on to his daughter Mrs. Dearie Mulvey. McKeever was the last of the three original co-owners of the team.

Larry MacPhail picked up the torch and ran with it. MacPhail went to work transforming the ballpark. Seats were repaired and painted blue along with the fences. Exits were painted bright orange. The grass was resodded with new turf and the stones and ruts were removed. The locker rooms and dugouts were refurbished. Concessions stands were added and bathrooms modernized. Even the press box was made more spacious and a press club was added back of the grandstand. To top it off, MacPhail added a lounge with a bar which pleased the sportswriters. It was often called "Larry's Sporting Lounge".

New, customer friendly ushers were hired and outfitted with green and gold uniforms. The players swapped their Kelly green uniforms for Dodger Blue. MacPhail then convinced Brooklyn Trust

Company to cough up another $100,000 for lights to play night baseball. He had a proven way to boost attendance from his Cincinnati days and this was it.

On Wednesday, June 15, 1938, MacPhail caught lightening in a bottle. The first night game brought out 38,748 fans and the fire department had to come to prevent more people from pouring in. Late arriving reserve seat holders had to literally fight for their seats from standing room fans who filled in empty spots during their absence. To hype the event, MacPhail had a fireworks show, a fife and drum band and Olympic medal winner Jesse Owens raced one of the Reds and Dodgers fastest players. Dodger Ernie Koy won the race with a ten yard handicap.

Larry's art deco lounge 1938

Just before the game started, starting Reds pitcher lefty Johnny Vander Meer was honored with a watch from his family and 700 well wishers from his hometown in Midland Park, New Jersey. Four days before, Vander Meer had thrown a no hitter against Boston at Crosley Field. Vander Meer then accomplished something never done before or since, he threw a second no hitter and Dodger fan Harry Rudolph was there. "I must have been six or seven years old and my father took me to the first night game at Ebbets Field". Johnny Vander Meer pitched his second no hitter and that's a record that's never been duplicated. Not too many people remember Ernie Koy either" Rudolph added. Koy, a part Indian, was usually greeted with a "woo, woo" chant. They did it when he'd come to bat or be in the field …the Dodger faithful would do it anytime," Rudolph said. Rudolph's father not only took him to Ebbets Field at an early age, he also provided a treat most kids could only dream about. "My father used to have baseball players over to the house. Dazzy Vance was a great Dodger pitcher and he used to be over at our house all the time. George Earnshaw from the Philadelphia A's used to come over too. My father was a great card player and they would all play cards," Rudolph. Rudolph would later become a Dodger batboy at the end of World War II. Another gimmick MacPhail used to improve attendance was to hire Babe Ruth as a coach midway through the 1938 season. Fans flocked to Ebbets Field to see Ruth take batting practice and smash lofty, fly balls over the right field wall and onto Bedford Ave. Ruth erroneously thought he was auditioning for a future managerial opening. He had made a pitch for becoming a Yankee manager but the general feeling was "he couldn't manage himself, how could he manage anyone else" so his overtures fell on deaf ears.

Meanwhile, Dodger Manager Grimes hadn't endeared himself to MacPhail during spring training when he told inquiring writers his squad would come in last. After they mentioned Philadelphia was still in the league, he amended his response by noting the Dodgers would probably finish in 7th place. MacPhail was not pleased and quickly had a meeting with Grimes and straightened him out. There was no more talk of where they would finish although Burleigh realized he was on thin ice for the rest of the season. Although the Dodgers only played seven night games, night baseball and other MacPhail innovations (like using dandelion yellow baseballs in a few games) helped double attendance from the 1937 total. However, Grimes' prediction held true and the Dodgers staggered home in 7th place.

Grimes did the best he could with what he had and even played peacemaker between Leo Durocher and Ruth when a fight was breaking out in the clubhouse one day after Durocher accused Ruth of not knowing the signs he was supposed to give as a coach. Grimes efforts weren't enough and he was sacked at the end of the World Series.

MacPhail decided Durocher (who had become the captain of the team) should play shortstop and manage his team. The move saved the team a few bucks but it also showed MacPhail's genius. He sensed Durocher was the inspirational firebrand who would lead his team to glory.

Fan Nat Muskin remembers Durocher. Muskin lived on Washington Avenue in Crown Heights. Two blocks behind his six-story apartment building was Ebbets Field." Every Saturday and Sunday morning, when the Dodgers were playing at home, all of us boys would walk to the big, marble rotunda and wait for Leo Durocher and the coaches to come to the ballpark," Muskin said.

"This was an important part of autograph collecting since the coaches would occasionally take baseballs from us (with our names), get them signed by the players in the locker room, and return then to us after the game. An indelible memory of Durocher during the late 1930"s was of him sweeping into the rotunda with his entourage dressed like a Hollywood personality," Muskin added.

Another thunderbolt was delivered in December when MacPhail announced that the Dodgers would broadcast their home games over the radio. The Giants and Yankees were livid with MacPhail because he was breaking a gentleman's agreement not to broadcast any home games "for free". The feeling was broadcasting home games would hurt attendance but MacPhail saw it as a way of gaining extra revenue (General Mills was the main sponsor paying $1,000 a game) and promoting his team at the same time. Mississippi born Red Barber was brought in from Cincinnati and was a hit with his folksy southern sayings and low key delivery on the radio.

Pre-game ceremony 1940

The 1939 season saw several key players added to the Dodgers as MacPhail got the Brooklyn Trust Company to get pitchers Whitlow Wyatt and Hugh Casey plus Dixie Walker. The club climbed to .500 and drew almost a million fans. Another baseball first for Ebbets Field was the initial television broadcast over NBC's W2XBS. With two cameras and Red Barber announcing the first game on August 26, the Dodgers played a doubleheader with the Reds in front of 33,535 fans and split the contests (winning the first game 6-2 and losing the second 5-1).

Barber did live, off the cuff commercials during the broadcast. One included slicing a banana and pouring milk over a bowl of Wheaties. Only several hundred television sets were tuned in but it was the beginning of sports broadcasting to the millions in later years.

Through out the whole season MacPhail and Durocher fought like dysfunctional lovers. MacPhail would fire Durocher for a variety of reasons and later forget about it (often after sobering up) or pretend it never happened. Their combustible personalities fueled numerous newspaper stories and seemed to propel the team.

Borough Hall pennant celebration 1941

The Dodgers finished in third place and made money for the first time in almost a decade while MacPhail's old team (the Cincinnati Reds) came in first place. In 1940, the Dodgers added two players dubbed "the gold dust twins". Harold "Pete" Reiser was obtained (he was declared a free agent by Commissioner Landis from Branch Rickey's farm system) and Harold "Pee Wee" Reese was bought from Boston's minor league system. MacPhail also picked up pitcher Kirbe Higbe, catcher Mickey Owen and outfielder Joe "Ducky" Medwick .Medwick quickly became a fan favorite. "My older sister was a rabid fan and she and her friends loved Medwick," said fan Jeanne Dolan. "When he arrived at the player's entrance at the field, he'd stretch both of his arms out and would walk into the field as many kids as he could fit within his outstretched arms. Needless to say, there was always a crowd of kids for him, "Dolan added.

Robert Ogden was a teenager when he first saw the Dodgers play. "There was nothing like the Bums in the late thirties and early forties," Ogden said. Ogden and a couple of his friends sneaked into Ebbets Field one day. "We got up to the top of the wall on the left field side and came up to the iron railing that arched out towards the street. We made it over the fence but not before I tore a new pair of pants. My mom could have killed me, "Ogden said. "What a thrill it was to see the likes of Dolph Camilli, Pete Reiser, Pee Wee Reese, Whitlow Wyatt, Kirby Higbe, Dixie Walker (the peeple's chere), Mickey Owen and the rest of dem bums. Dolph Camilli was Ogden's favorite player. "He wore number 4 which is my favorite number to this day," said Ogden.

Another innovation MacPhail came up with on May 7, 1940 was air travel. The Dodgers flew two planes home to Brooklyn's Floyd Bennett Field from Chicago. It turned out to be a gala event when over 10,000 fans showed up after midnight and Borough President John Cashmore gave a welcoming speech.

September brought a different type of excitement when MacPhail invited some former Dodgers back for an old timers' game. Zack Wheat, Dazzy Vance and former manager Bill Dahlen (first manager at Ebbets Field) were among the many stars who played in the game. Another game on September 16 brought out the worst in a Dodger fan after Durocher was ejected and the Dodgers had just lost an extra inning game to the league leading Reds. Six foot, three inch umpire George Magerkurth was walking off the field when a short, stocky 200 pound, 21 year old parolee named Frank Germano jumped out of the stands and started pummeling him at home plate. Another startled umpire Bill Stewart pulled Germano off Magerkurth and Frank was shipped back to jail but not before a photographer snapped his picture pounding Magerkurth. Magerkurth later declined to press charges against the fan. The Dodgers moved up to second place and finished twelve games behind the Reds.

In 1941 all the pieces fell into place after Billy Herman was brought over from the Cubs early in the season. MacPhail was also busy with another innovation- the batting helmet. His plastic protective liner for baseball hats was devised by Johns Hopkins doctors in the spring after Joe Medwick and Pee Wee Reese had been beaned the previous year. MacPhail wanted to protect his valuable assets and give him an edge. The Dodgers drew over a million (1,037,765) for the first time since 1930 and got their first pennant since 1920 on September 25. Brooklyn had a big celebration

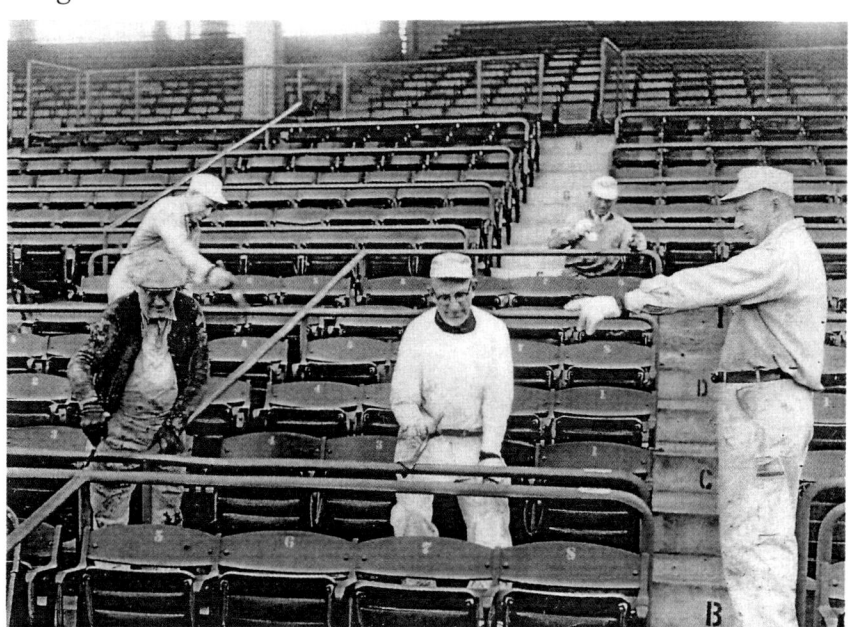

Paint job for Ebbets

with players riding in a motorcade from Grand Army Plaza to Borough Hall. There were a million people jamming downtown. Bob Ogden was the Borough President John Cashmore's paperboy in 1941 and he can be seen in a photo behind New York Mayor O'Dwyer in the crowd with the National League Champion Dodgers on the steps of Borough Hall. "I was on the reviewing stand because that was the usual time I delivered his (Cashmore's) daily Brooklyn Eagle and I was invited to the stand by his male secretary," Ogden said.

The joyous fans would soon be sobered up by cross borough rival Yankees in the first Dodger World Series since 1920. Down two games to one at Ebbets Field, the Dodgers were leading the Yanks with one out to go when pitcher Hugh Casey's third strike on Tommy Henrich sailed by catcher Mickey Owen's glove. Henrich was safe at first and the Yankees rallied to beat the Dodgers 7 to 4.

The Yankees closed out the series the next day with a 3 to 1 victory and the Brooklyn Eagle exclaimed in a headline Wait Until Next Year. It was a phrase Ebbets Field fans would use over and over for years. Spring training took place in Havana and Daytona Beach in 1942. World War II hadn't affected the Dodgers yet. The team was loose and gambling was commonplace among the players. Taking the biggest gamble were Pee Wee Reese and Pete Reiser who got married at the same time. MacPhail took a dim view of their romantic duel marriage and felt the pennant flew out the window when they said their vows.

The Dodgers were a cocky and confident team after winning the 1941 pennant. They were without a doubt the most hated team in the league too. Previous beanball wars, Durocher's bench jockeying that rubbed off on his players and the raucous fans at Ebbets Field got under opponent's skins. It was the edge the Dodgers often needed and they used it to full advantage.

As the 1942 season started, MacPhail had suggested two All Star games be played to benefit the war effort. Marian, his daughter, also suggested to her father that they put an organ in Ebbets Field. He brushed her off but the next time she came to Ebbets Field, Gladys Gooding was playing an organ there. Gooding was also the answer to the question of "who was the only person to play for the baseball Dodgers, the hockey Rangers and basketball Knicks"?

The Dodger Sym-Phoney was also formed among a motley group of five fans from the Williamsburg section of Brooklyn. They roamed the stands and played their snare drum, cymbals, trumpet and bass drum to the fans delight and opposing player's dismay.

On May 8.1942, the first of 16 games to be played (one at each major league stadium) for the benefit of service organizations was held at Ebbets Field. MacPhail outdid himself by selling 42,822 tickets to the event. He did this by having everyone from the sportswriters, players, umpires, Western Union operators and even employees of the Dodgers buy their own tickets to get into the game.

MacPhail contracted the Navy Relief Society to be the official promoter of the game for tax purposes. This was done to maximize the amount available to the relief effort. Over $60,000 was donated to the organizations from this game alone.

There was a pre-game parade of midshipmen, their officers, bluejackets and American Legion standard bearers. A variety of military bands played during a parade at Ebbets Field as well. Brooklyn tenor Everrett Clark led the crowd in the singing of God Bless America followed by the audience recitation of the pledge of allegiance. The Dodgers went on to beat the N.Y. Giants 7-6 in the first regulation twilight game (night ball was now forbidden because of the wartime blackouts).

For much of the year, the Dodgers led the standings but MacPhail sensed they were overconfident. He confronted his team in the locker room but after Dixie Walker offered to bet him they would win by eight games, he backed off. The Dodgers did win four more games in 1942 than in 1941 but the Cardinals came in first place with 106 wins. MacPhail in the meantime decided to join the army and serve his country. The Brooklyn Trust Company appreciated the fact that the team's debt was paid off, improvements had been made to Ebbets Field and their minor league teams were flourishing but they also saw MacPhail's own personal salary grow to the highest in the league and there was little leftover for themselves.

The colorful and flashy dressing MacPhail had offended many with his loud mouth and obnoxious manners. Many felt he was one step ahead of the posse in his leaving town. Taking his place was a man who seemed to be totally the opposite of him …Branch Rickey.

Chapter 5   War Years & the Rickey Revolution

Jackie Robinson

Bushy browed Branch Rickey wore rumpled, baggy clothes, never swore (except for the phrase "Judas Priest") or drank liquor. He was a religious man who could quote scripture as easily as any modern evangelist and was a tight fisted man with the team's purse strings.

Rickey had been an elementary school teacher before going to Ohio Wesleyan University (where he played football and baseball). After a stint in the Texas League, Rickey made it to Cincinnati as a catcher in 1904. After they discovered he wouldn't play baseball on Sundays (for religious reasons), he was released. He played on the St. Louis Browns and New York Highlanders (later Yankees) with little success and retired with a sore arm. Having thirteen bases stolen on him in one game convinced him it was time to go in 1907.

He married an Ohio merchant's daughter Jane Moulton and got a law degree at University of Michigan. After practicing law in Idaho, he returned to U of M and coached the baseball team. He also did some part time scouting for the St Louis Browns.

He rejoined the Browns in 1913 and was assistant to the president, manager and business manager at different times while there until 1917 when he became president of the St. Louis Cardinals.

After serving in the war, Rickey returned to become manager. and continued to work in the front office at the same time. He was fired as manager but became general manager and through necessity he developed the minor league farm system so many future executives would envy and try and emulate over the years.

The Cardinals won six pennants and four World Series plus they stockpiled talent through Rickey's rein between 1925 and 1942. At its peak, there were almost a thousand players and fifty teams available to Rickey. Stockholders were paid an 8% dividend on their investment each year for fifteen years while Rickey ran the Cardinals. He was rewarded with a salary of $50,000 plus another $30,000 in bonuses and commissions. Cardinal owner Sam Breadon and Rickey finally parted ways after the 1942 season. Some thought Breadon was jealous of Rickey's accomplishments and making too much money for a job he figured he could now do himself. Rickey quickly joined his son Branch Rickey Jr., (who was serving as MacPhail's farm director) in Brooklyn and at the age of 61 became president of the Dodgers.

World War II saw an exodus of everyday players to the service. Within two years, the Dodgers had lost Hugh Casey, Pee Wee Reese, Pete Reiser, Larry French, Kirby Higbe and Billy Herman to the army plus Arky Vaughn and Dolph Camilli to retirement. Branch Rickey had to make do with limited resources. Fans had to make do also with a lower quality product on the field too. "Baseball during the war years (1942-1945) was comprised of 4-f's, old men and youngsters. Names that come to mind were Tom (Buckshot) Brown (15 year old shortstop), Eddie Basinski (a concert musician of either violin or cello as best I remember and a wearer of thick spectacles), Bobo Newsom (a character), and Frenchy Bordagary (a mustached colorful player) who played the infield or outfield. To my memory none of the war-time players made an impact and none were on the team of 1947," said fan Bob Gottdenker. Joseph MacDougall grew up in Prospect Heights not too far from Ebbets Field, "One of the few opportunities I had to go there (financial constraints) during the early 40's was the day of a scrap metal drive to aid the war effort," MacDougall said. "The price of admission was any piece of metal. As I remember, I had a key to contribute and that was my key to admission," MacDougall said. "I do recall a long line of men and boys hefting the darnedest collection of metal objects: automobile bumpers, other auto parts, bed springs and many other unidentifiable pieces," he said. "What I'll always remember is the sight of the field itself, such an expanse of well-manicured green grass with the infield cut into it. I also remember the sounds…the noise from the roar of the crowd when something eventful happened and the crisp sound of a bat hitting a well hit ball," MacDougall said.

Over sixty years have passed since Fred Nash first saw the Dodgers. "I was eight years old when I went to my first game at Ebbets Field in 1941. It seems like yesterday that I heard Gladys Gooding playing the Dodgers theme-Follow the Dodgers. She was also the organ player at Madison Square Garden," Nash recalled. "I was at War Bond games during World War II where I saw Babe Ruth exhibit his hitting. The vendors had peanuts, hot dogs, crackerjacks and beer plus there was the knot hole gang where kids were given free tickets to the bleachers. The talent that the Dodgers had during the war was second hand. Howie Schultz 1b, Eddie Stanky 2b, Edie Basinski ss, Dixie Walker rf, Goody Rosen cf, John Dantonio c, are some of the players I remember," Nash added. "During the war, my fiancé and I went to a game and I began to pay for two seats…"No! No!" said the gatekeepers and they directed me to a nearby entrance where service folks got in for free. Nice gesture," said John Nichols Jeanne Dolan was able to get into Ebbets Field another way "During the war, we were urged to render fat from cooking. It was used in the manufacture of ammunition, I believe. Days were set aside at Ebbets Field where you were admitted for something like 10 or 15 cents if you brought a one pound can of rendered fat. I saw many games based on that entry fee," Dolan added.

On Saturday, July 10, 1943, 4,500 women brought at least a half pound of fat on Kitchen Fats Day and were offered free grandstand seats at Ebbets Field. The fat was converted into glycerin which was a key ingredient in making explosives.

Lee Mead was a boy during World War II but he went to every home game one year. "During World War II, anyone who brought 10 pounds of scrap metal (for the war effort) would get into

Trolley dodger c/o Joseph Saitta, Trolley works

Ebbets Field for free. I cleared out every lot in Sheepshead Bay," said Mead. "I couldn't get on the subway with the metal, so I had to walk along the BMT Brighton line from Sheepshead Bay to Prospect Park and back again. The wartime Dodgers were terrible but so were the other teams. It didn't matter …it was still the Dodgers," Mead said.

Bob Gottdenker remembers Leo Durocher during the war years. "In those days, ballplayers rode the subway system but Leo came to the park via motor transportation-taxi or someone driving him. One Sunday morning (1942 or 1943) along came Leo Durocher, who was serving a one week suspension. He took another kid and I into the park with him, gave us each $1.00 to spend and let us sit in a box with him and watch a game. What a thrill for a 12 year old. Leo was a great dresser, wore a ring, was bald and I thought he was God," Gottdenker recalls. Dodger batboy, at the time, Harry Rudolph thought Durocher was "a lovely guy…he was my hero. He was married to actress Lorraine Day at the time. Whenever I did anything for him, he always gave me a five dollar tip. His voice was so commanding and could hypnotize me," Rudolph fondly said.

L. Durocher & D. Walker give boat to B. Rickey in 1946

While this was going on, Branch Rickey had his scouts touring the country and signing as many young prospects as possible. Other teams were cutting back expenses but Rickey wanted to get a jump on them when the war was over. At one point, Rickey mailed 20,000 letters to coaches throughout the country asking for recommendations.

The 1943 season had two events happen that would shape the future of Ebbets Field and society in general. The first event was New York's legislature created the Ives-Quinn Law, which was to prevent discrimination in hiring practices. Mayor Fiorello La Guardia publicly pleaded with all three New York baseball teams to drop their ban on black ballplayers.

The second event was Branch Rickey's decision to find a black ballplayer to desegregate major league baseball. Rickey got Brooklyn Trust's George McLaughlin's approval to seek out the best talent available and that it may include a "negro player or two". There was also another growing problem Rickey that inherited …gambling. Rickey reined in the full blown gambling on the team that caught the eye of baseball Commissioner Landis. Coach Charlie Dressen was dismissed (later rehired at a loss of salary) and the message was sent that high stakes poker games on team trips were verboten. Manager Leo Durocher had to hold card games to a 15 cent limit.

In the meantime, the Dodgers were finishing third in 1943, seventh in 1944 and third in 1945. The 1944 season was so bad that the Dodgers had two pitchers that could only see out of one eye, a shortstop that was missing a kidney and a variety of discharged wounded veterans. Of the fifty three players on the roster that year, twenty were making their major league debuts.

The most exciting thing to happen at Ebbets Field that year was in the form of an exhibition game against the Philadelphia Phillies for the Red Cross. Frank Sinatra sang three songs at home plate for swooning bobbysoxers and the Dodgers beat the Phillies 13-11 in a game that netted the Red Cross over $14,000. Sinatra, who sang "Take Me out To the Ballgame," "Let Me Call You Sweetheart" and "People Will Say We're In Love," was joined by baseball funny man Al Schacht and Babe Ruth at the benefit.

Rickey's old team, the St. Louis Cardinals won another championship over hometown rival St. Louis Browns. He was now in competition with his own Frankenstein.

Outfielder Gene Hermanski

In November, Ed McKeever's heirs sold their 25 per cent of the club to a group that included Branch Rickey and the team's lawyer Walter O'Malley, They also picked up the other shares from the Ebbets' heirs as well. No longer would there be a stalemate in the front office because of feuding between the McKeever and Ebbets' heirs. Dearie Mulvey and her husband Jim held the remaining shares (25%) in the Dodgers.

The 1944 season also saw the passing of the man who "cleaned up' the game of baseball. Commissioner Kenesaw Mountain Landis restored the integrity of the sport after the Black Sox betting scandal in 1920 but he also never lifted a finger while blacks were systematically excluded from major league baseball.

In the spring of 1945, Rickey announced the creation of the United States League and that the Negro Brooklyn Brown Dodgers would play at Ebbets Field. Only 2,000 fans showed up for the first game on May 24th when the Brown Dodgers beat the Hilldale club of Philadelphia 3-2. Attendance never picked up and the new league never challenged the Negro leagues and was finished after the season was over. The league was later seen as a cover for Rickey to find the man to change baseball.

Rickey saw an opportunity with Landis gone and had a scout Clyde Sukeforth follow multi talented, star athlete Jackie Robinson through most of the 1945 season while he played for the Kansas City Monarchs (in the Negro Leagues). He wanted to know not only if Robinson had the talent but if he could handle the pressure involved in breaking the color barrier of baseball. When verbal and possible physical abuse would be heaped on him, Rickey said. "I'm looking for some one with the courage not to fight back".

Branch Rickey needed a rich, untapped source of talent to compete with his former team and others like the Cubs (who would win the pennant in 1945). It was also a personal goal of his to integrate baseball since he witnessed discrimination first hand while as a Ohio Wesleyan baseball coach in 1904. Charles Thomas was the only black player on his team and was denied a room at the Oliver Hotel when Rickey's squad arrived in South Bend, Indiana to play Notre Dame. Rickey got into a discussion with the hotel manager and after much negotiation and many heated words, Thomas was allowed to stay in Rickey's room with an extra cot installed there. During a meeting with the team captain in the room, Rickey noticed an upset and shaken Thomas crying and clawing at his hands saying "Black skin, black skin. If I could only make 'em white". Thomas made it through the season and eventually became a dentist in New Mexico. The incident however haunted Rickey for years and it was one reason he felt morally compelled to help integrate baseball.

Jackie Robinson played for the Dodger's top farm club (Montreal Royals) in 1946 and he helped them win their championship. He also made the International League's All Star team and won the batting title with a .349 average. Even though he missed more than two dozen games, Robinson led the league in walks and runs scored.

The Dodgers, meanwhile in 1946, battled the Cardinals, and everyone else all season long. Two games in late May with the Chicago Cubs at Ebbets Field provided plenty of fisticuffs for the fans to enjoy. Cubs Len Merullo, who had fought with Dodgers Eddie Stanky the day before, got into a heated exchange with Pee Wee Reese during batting practice. Tempers flared and Dixie Walker of the Dodgers charged Merullo and they tumbled on the ground with fists flying. Both teams joined in and after 25 policemen separated the players, order was restored with Walker missing a tooth.

The Dodgers won the game in extra innings as Reese's sacrifice fly knocked in Pete Reiser who had earlier tripled. The win deadlocked the Bums with the Cardinals for the league lead. National League President Ford Frick fined Walker $150 and suspended him for five days. Reese was fined $100 and Murello fined $150 and suspended for eight days. Cubs Phil Caverretta was fined $100 and coach Red Smith $100 and a five game suspension. Cubs General Manager Jimmy Gallagher was livid. "Regardless of what Frick says or the league rules which state a player must pay his own fine, the Chicago club will pay the player's fines," Gallagher said. Gallagher added he was proud of what Merullo did. "I said to him 'Len, if you hadn't punched back at him, I'd have fined you $500'. Those Brooklyn rowdies have been asking for it for a long time. You can't take that stuff from them forever, "Gallagher said.

Ebbets Field rotunda

The Dodgers and Cardinals continued their back and forth fight for first place and settled their differences with a first ever playoff to end the season. The Cards won two games by a score of 4-2 in St. Louis and 8-4 at Ebbets Field to take the crown. Although Branch Rickey was called "El Cheapo" by newsman Jimmy Powers and others, he gave every member of the team which included the manager, coaches and traveling secretary a new Studebaker automobile for their effort in 1946. The players in return chipped in and bought Rickey a Chris Craft boat and presented it to him at Ebbets Field. The one element that would have given them the edge in 1946 was north of the border, Durocher had begged Rickey for Robinson to be promoted but Rickey turned him down. After spending the entire spring training of 1947 with Montreal, Jackie Robinson was promoted to the Dodgers on April 9 (six days before the opener). Harry Rudolph was the Dodger batboy that day.

"The Montreal team came in to play an exhibition game at Ebbets Field. Jackie Robinson was on the Montreal team. The game ended and I was busy getting all the bats in a big trunk, the catcher's equipment, sunglasses and all the paraphernalia out of the dugout. "Then I carted it back with a dolly. The dugout came up to the steps and there was a long breezeway and a fence that separated the fans from the ball field. As I got near the clubhouse, I saw a lot of lights. There were all these cameras (like the eyes and ears of the world) on tripods and they had just announced that Jackie Robinson was coming up with the team. It was amazing, I could hardly get into the clubhouse," Rudolph remembers. Rudolph grew up in New York and didn't think too much about a black man coming on the team. However, "when he (Robinson) went on the road it was a different thing". "The southern guys didn't treat him too well, Dixie Walker, Ed Stanky and those guys. But Pee Wee Reese, he treated him well," Rudolph said.

Brooklyn outfielder Gene Hermanski was also there during that time at Ebbets Field. "He (Robinson) played against us. He never played with the Dodgers but he was with Montreal and drew big crowds in the spring training. Course he went to Montreal and spent a whole year there and made MVP (he really finished 5th in the voting) and they brought him up in 1947," Hermanski said. "I didn't think too much of it because I was a northerner, grew up in New Jersey. But I heard rumbling from some of the southerners, Kirby Higbe, Dixie Walker, Hugh Casey and one or two others you know? They wanted to protest, but you know I was just a kid comin' up so, I didn't give a damn what they were thinking," Hermanski added. In Jackie Robinson's opening game, Hermanski knocked him in for his first big league run. "We won that game 3-1 against Johnny Sain. He was with the Braves". Hermanski takes pride in his role in the 1947 opener. He is one of only two people still alive in that starting lineup.

John "Spider" Jorgenson is the other player and he remembers Jackie Robinson fondly. Jorgenson was on Montreal club with Robinson in spring training. "I had a pretty good spring and a good series against the Dodgers and (Cookie) Lavagetto and Arky Vaughan got hurt and they couldn't play so they brought me up. I didn't expect to play but they said to get over to the office at 10:00 in the morning," he said.

"We were at the McAlpin hotel in New York and we got there and they hemmed and hawed around and they finally rushed me out to the ballpark. I didn't have any equipment. All my stuff had gone to Syracuse where we (Montreal) were to open up. I had to borrow Jackie Robinson's glove. He played first base that day so I used his second base glove. I used Ray Blades spikes …and this that and the other thing and all of a sudden I'm in the lineup batting 6th," Jorgenson said.

Jorgenson played along side of Robinson that year and hit .274 in 129 games. "I liked Ebbets Field. For some reason the blue background…the ballpark…I could see the ball better. I don't know why but the Ebbets Field background was better than the Polo Grounds , Cincinnati or Philadelphia's," he said. Jorgenson's nickname came from high school. "I was a skinny guy and wore black and orange trunks at a basketball game. We played skins and shirts and a teacher came in and asked 'Who is the guy in the black and orange trunks'? "He looks like a black widow spider in those trunks, just like the one I uncovered in my woodpile last Saturday', and it (the nickname) stuck with me," Jorgenson added.

Teammate Don Lund was also right there when he saw history being made in 1947. "Jackie and I were with the AAA farm team Montreal Royals. We played the Dodgers down in Cuba and then at the end of spring training we had a ball game on a weekend (at Ebbets Field) just before Montreal was to go to Syracuse to open the season. "I had one of them spring trainings I should have saved for every year. I had something like 12 homeruns and one of them was off Ralph Branca in Ebbets Field," said Lund. "So the next day, they bought "Spider" Jorgenson (who was a third baseman) and Robinson's contract and my contract…instead of going to Syracuse we went with the Dodgers to open the season," Lund added.

Lund was taken aback at the treatment Robinson received. "It was just awful some of the things that were said to him. You just couldn't believe it, really. But he kept his cool and it was unbelievable that he could because there were some really derogatory remarks," Lund said "And then he showed them he could play. He had the ability to disrupt the game, to take an extra base, then fake and go ahead and steal. He struggled at the very beginning and I'm sure with the pressure and all that, but then all of a sudden he started to go," Lund said. Fireballing pitcher Rex Barney in Mike Bryan's Baseball Lives described his first experiences with Jackie Robinson. "That year (1947) I also pitched the first major-league game

Jackie Robinson ever played in. I had gone to a Jesuit High School, Creighton Prep, and then Creighton University, and we played with and against blacks and thought nothing about it. In 1946 there were rumors that Jackie was going to join the club. He was in Montreal at the time. We had several rednecks on our club who swore they'd never play with a black player. Lo and behold, the day before Opening Day in 1947, Jackie joined our club as a first baseman. Utter chaos. Terrible. He was a super human being, had to be, and of course Mr. Rickey knew this. He had researched the whole thing and Jackie was the guy they chose. A lot of guys could never have survived," Barney said.

The Dodgers set an all time attendance record in Robinson's first year with 1,807,526 fans flocking to see the phenomenon of the first black star leading his team to a pennant. It was a love affair between Robinson and the hometown fans. To fan Barry Becher, Jackie Robinson was the most exciting player he ever saw. "He was a force in all the games I attended. The fans loved him," Becher said. "When he came up to bat, everyone would be on their feet. If he got on base, he would drive the pitchers crazy by taking long leads and dancing off the bases. "To this day, I have never seen anyone take a lead like Jackie did. His stance was very different than anyone else's. His hands were held very high, up near his face," Becher said.

There was no race issue among us kids because we were too young to know any difference. Jackie was our hero. He was one of a kind and had more guts than just about anybody. He broke down more barriers than anyone realizes. He was the greatest," Becher added. For Charles Tierney, as a eleven or twelve year old, "the most popular player there (Ebbets Field) without a doubt was Jackie Robinson." "I mean he just came and he just owned the fans…because he was so dynamic. The things he did on the ball field. I mean I would watch him, a soft line drive would be hit into left field and he'd be on first base and he'd go nice and gingerly into second. As soon as the left fielder released an arching throw into shortstop, he'd take off for third," Tierney said. "I mean 'Wow' look at what this guy does. Robinson would slide in, he'd get up and the first thing he would be doing is see if the guy that hit the ball is going into second. That's the kind of brains, a baseball mind the guy had. He was just a phenomenal talent. Knew the game inside and out," Tierney marveled. Fan Steve Levine thinks Jackie Robinson was the most important player in baseball. "Robinson's skills were considerable and in some areas bordered on the remarkable. "He hit for average, had reasonable power and was an agile, sure handed fielder. On the bases, he had no peer. He may not have been the best ballplayer I ever saw but he was without doubt the greatest competitor," Levine said.

Even opposing team's fans were amazed at Jackie Robinson's impact on the game. "The Yankees and Dodgers used to play a preseason game every year," Yankee fan Michael Brozinsky recalls. "On one occasion our dad took us to the game at Ebbets Field and we were seated behind third base. Jackie Robinson had gotten to third base and was taking his lead back and forth and back and forth. "The crowd was going absolutely crazy. This was the most exciting thing this lifelong Yankee fan has ever seen and I'm sure many who were there that day would agree," Brozinsky said. "No ball was hit, no catch was made and nothing had to happen. Anticipation based on past steals of home by Jackie took over the minds and hearts of all the fans. I don't remember what finally happened but how many other players excited the Dickens out of a stadium by just taking a lead? "Brozinsky marveled.

After a slow start, Robinson progressed to become the Rookie of the Year in 1947. He had a .297 batting average and led the Dodgers in runs (125), singles (127) and total bases (255) plus he tied Pee Wee Reese in homers with 12. He led the National League in stolen bases (29) and did it all while suffering housing discrimination on the road as well as racial taunts and abuse from opposing players and fans.

He was honored at Jackie Robinson Day on September 23 at Ebbets Field, the day after the Dodgers captured their first pennant since 1941. Over 26,000 fans turned out to see the newly crowned National League Champions and give tribute to new hero Jackie Robinson. Among the gifts Robinson received that day were a brand new auto, a gold watch, a radio and television set, a gold pencil and pen set, silverware and cutlery, an electric broiler and a check. The Amsterdam News also presented Robinson with a plaque for his contribution to "interracial goodwill". Among the many speakers there was entertainer Bill (Bojangles) Robinson who mused, "I'm 69 years old but I never thought I'd live to see the day when I'd stand face to face with Ty Cobb in Technicolor." Jackie Robinson thanked everyone especially "the members of the Dodger team who were so cooperative in helping me improve my game."

It hadn't been easy. Burt Shotton guided Robinson through the season after Leo Durocher was suspended as manager for a year by new Baseball Commissioner Happy Chandler for conduct detrimental to baseball just as the season as to begin. Durocher had put down a budding revolt in spring training by some players who didn't like the possibility of having a black teammate. By the time the season was over, even a redneck like Dixie Walker had to give Robinson grudging respect for his talent.

In spite of heroics by Cookie Lavagetto breaking up Bill Bevens attempt at a World Series no hitter in Game 4 and Al Gionfriddo's circus catch off Joe Dimaggio's bat to preserve a victory in Game 6, the Dodgers were beaten by the Yankees 4 games to three in the World Series but baseball would never be the same.

On December 10, 1947 a headline in the Sporting News read …L.A VS BALTIMORE IN BIDS FOR BROWNS. No baseball franchise had moved in over 40 years at that point but this headline would prove to be ominous to Dodger fans and Ebbets Field. That same week, Leo Durocher's return to the Dodgers was announced. The Reverend Vincent J. Powell, the Brooklyn Diocesan director of the Catholic Youth Organization, withdrew his objections to Durocher's return if he towed the moral line. The group had previously withdrawn their participation in the Knot Hole Gang which let youth organizations into Dodger games for free. Things were looking up for the Dodgers in 1948.

Chapter 6   Fans in the Stands

Typical young fan in 1950's

Jackie Robinson's arrival coincided with other players coming through the Dodger farm system or via trades to the big league club. Pitcher Preacher Roe and third sacker Billy Cox came over in the Dixie Walker trade with the Pirates in December of 1947. Pitchers Carl Erskine and Rex Barney joined outfielders Carl Furillo and Eugene (Duke) Snider with catcher Roy Campanella to help form the new blood that would join with holdovers like Pee Wee Reese and Gil Hodges to become The Boys Of Summer (coined by Roger Kahn in his best seller).

These players would create the glory years at Ebbets Field from the late 40's to mid 50's. Many players lived in the neighborhoods around Ebbets Field during the season and their accessibility on and off the field endeared them to Dodger fans.

The fans themselves were knowledgeable, good natured, rowdy, loud, sarcastic, encouraging and loyal. Here are some of their stories.

Jim Gaffey started going to Ebbets Field when he was 6 years old with his dad in 1949. "Just a wonderful feeling to walk through the cool section below stadium and then to walk up the ramp and out into the sunlight and see the field stretch out before you. "It was magical," Gaffey said.

"Later when we were old enough to cross major streets with the gang, we would line up outside of the bleacher entrance. Many groups would be coming in buses to bring "their" kids to a game. There were always left over tickets and the ushers and organizations would allow us to tag along at the end of the line to see the game. "We always thought this was fun to enter one day with the YMCA, then next with CYO, then Hadassah, then Boys Club, then NAACP. "It did not matter. We were all the same…we had a uniform (white T-shirt, jeans with holes in our knees and old US Keds with broken laces tied in knots). We didn't care…we were in Ebbets Field," Gaffey recalled.

Carl Prince, author of Brooklyn's Dodgers, got to experience Ebbets Field etiquette up close and personal when he was 13 years old. "In May or June 1948, I went to Ebbets Field early as always to watch batting practice. Willard 'Willie the Knuck' Ramsdell, a journeyman pitcher, was just coming towards the bullpen after shagging flies; I shoved my scorecard at him, yelling at him to sign. As he passed, he told me to f**k off and kept going. Unfortunately he shouted it and a bunch of fans (who arrived early to be properly lubricated by game time) heard him. As he got to the bullpen (very close to the field and mostly unprotected in the appallingly small ballpark) they started chanting almost in unison, 'Willie the Knuck, you f**k, sign the kid's ball. Willie the Knuck …' etc. He took off from the bullpen for the dugout, leaving the chanting fans in the dust…and didn't sign my scorecard. I have been haunted by this memory ever since and it has scarred me forever". Carl was kidding, I think.

According to Bob Karasik, "the Dodger clubhouse was along Empire Blvd. (first baseline). Bathrooms had windows that opened up to the street. Regulars, like myself, knew where they were located. We would hand self addressed 2 cent postcards blindly through the window to a receiving hand.

Ebbets Field

Had no clue to whom it was attached to. We would have it returned with an autograph of that player or receive a 'great' surprise in the mail in a few days," Karasik said. "I lived across the street from Ebbets Field (1953-1960)" Elaine Friedman Nugent said. "I remember meeting Red Barber in the local drug store buying cough syrup. "I also saw President Eisenhower leaving the ball park in an open convertible waving to the crowds. That was exciting… and the most exciting thing was the Dodgers beat the Yankees in the World Series of 1955," recalls Nugent "I remember when I was young there was a bus parked outside Ebbets and it had a big banner saying Brooklyn Dodgers," Robert

Knot-hole gang membership card

Lerner said. "So, all the kids handed our pads up to the players inside and they all signed them. When they returned them to us they all had names we never heard of before and we ripped them up. Some people on the bus got off and chased us down the block. We found out later they were the Brooklyn Dodgers football team," said Robert Lerner. "A friend of mine was an infant in a carriage and his sister had taken him over to Ebbets Field to see the ballplayers. They were on Bedford Ave. (which was a hill) and she let go of the carriage to get an autograph and the carriage was rolling down the hill when Cookie Lavagetto chased the carriage and saved my friend from a disaster. Cookie was his hero and his sister's too," according to Robert Lerner.

Fan Club at Ebbets

Mike Casey Kocijan, son of Dodger great Hugh Casey was "4 or 5" when his aunt took him to the ballpark. "I remember her telling me to "Stand and clap…stand and clap. I had no idea what was going on and I couldn't even see the field," he said. "But it struck me that is how Ebbets Field was back in those days…it wasn't a very big place but everybody kind of knew everybody," said Casey Kocijan "It was kind of a phenomenon, it was a multicultural racial planet…all these people from every walk of background came together for the Dodgers," Casey Kocijan said. "I attended many pro football games before and after World War II. High School games were played there (at Ebbets Field)… Erasmus vs. Manual was big then," John Nichols said. "Sid Luckman must have been in one of those games before going on to Columbia University and pro football stardom," said Nichols.

"Ebbets Field was very warm and cozy. We spent most of our time in the bleachers but were treated just as well as the box seat patrons. One really felt at home there and you could go with the guys or even feel comfortable taking a date there," noted Stan Field "During the early and mid fifties when I was dating my wife to be, a bunch of us used to go to the games together and even if there were some guys without dates we felt very comfortable. The thing that sticks out in my mind most about Ebbets Field was the friendly atmosphere between fans and other fans and fans and the players. I remember one incident when we were sitting in the bleachers during batting practice," Field noted. "The Pirates George Metkovitch was out in center catching a few when one of us taped a pen to a "Spaldeen" and threw it onto the field. George picked it up, untaped the pen, signed the ball and threw it back to us. Today, you just about have to buy an autograph," said Stan Field. "As a street smart New Yorker, I soon learned that it was easy to get into most games for free. I would go to Montgomery Street and quietly attach myself to the back of one of the group lineups and proceed into the ballpark," Alan Greenberg said. "Not being satisfied with a left field grandstand seat, I would slowly but surely make my way to the infield area upstairs. After a few innings, I would scout out the lower deck from upstairs, zero in on a vacant seat and make my way down. By the late innings when people started to leave I would make another move, this time to the field boxes for the end of the game," Greenberg said. "When the game ended, I had the ultimate thrill because the box level fans were allowed to go on the field and exit through centerfield, the very same outfield patrolled by the Duke. The fact that I lived in the exact opposite direction didn't matter. Leaving Ebbets Field through centerfield could put any kid in a field of dreams," Alan Greenberg remembers. "I remember going to the ballpark and waiting with perhaps 90 other kids at a gate, hoping to be picked as a turnstile boy. Pay was 50 cents but you could watch the game (this was when there was no school and game time was 3 pm.). "I also remember getting a running start and hurdling a turnstile getting admission to the ballpark," Bob Gottdenker said. "The third day in a row I did this, I was chased by the park police, caught and had people in the stands booing the police. I was brought into an office and faced big, tough Joe Moore the head officer. He took my name, telephone number and school I attended. I was in constant fear of getting in school and home trouble for 30 days. "I was 12 at the time," Bob Gottdenker said. "I also joined several of my friends on a roof top on Bedford Ave. The right field scoreboard obstructed some of our view and watching of the game," Gottdenker adds.

Paul Warner has some funny remembrances of Ebbets Field. Like the one that happened at a day game (when he was about nine) after his mom had just gotten a beer for herself and soda for him. "We were seated way down the leftfield line, deep in foul territory under the rafters…the cheap seats. "I don't think my mom had taken two sips of beer when…plop… a pigeon had dropped a direct hit into her beer cup! The folks behind us saw it and they were hysterical. After a while, mom started laughing too," Warner said.

Charles Tierney listened to all the Dodger games and knew all the players so when he was nine and his dad asked him what he wanted for his birthday, he told him, "I want to go to a Dodger's game". "We didn't have tickets so we went up and got two box seats (left field boxes maybe second or third row). I remember sitting out there and baking in the sun and it was hot. I was very fair and I burn easily so we bought these here cardboard sun visors for our heads. They were like 50 cents apiece and the seats were $2.50. The Dodgers were playing the Cardinals and I remember Musial had about 5 or 6 hits (in a Saturday afternoon doubleheader).

The next year, when he was ten, Tierney took public transportation to the park and got in by jumping into line for a chance to be on the Happy Felton show. During one trip, he saw Tommy Lasorda pitch. "I remember one day (it was a rain out game) there were maybe a few thousand people in the stands and I wiggled my way behind home plate and I watched him (Lasorda) pitch. I said, 'This guy's unhittable'. The ball was bouncing up and down. I don't know what the hell he was throwing. So it started to rain and during the rain delay I went down to the bullpen dugout," Tierney said. "I believe it was Joe Black (relief pitcher for the Dodgers) and I got into a conversation with him. Me a kid! I said 'Wow, this guy is so good but if he could put the ball over the plate, he'd be a star. His problem was he could not find the plate," Tierney said. "I would go around the ballpark and look for empty seats about the fourth inning. I'd always find an empty seat and you'd get into a conversation and it didn't matter whether I was ten or eleven years old. I knew all there was to know about the game at that point and I would have conversations with people I didn't really know', Tierney added.

"The stories with my dad had to be before I was seven," said Danny Wolfe "I can remember going to Ebbets Field with my dad and distinctly remember being on the third base side. I couldn't figure why I was cheering for the Dodgers but not for the other team (I guess that's being young at heart, with no hatred)," he said. "After the games, I remember coming home with dad and Gil (Hodges) he

Schaeffer Scoreboard & right field wall

dropping us off on New York Ave. between Foster and Farraguat Rd. He was my dad's friend (probably best friend) because I hear so many stories about the Dodgers and my family. Either my sister or her friend dated Chuck Connors (the Rifleman) when he played for the Bums. My dad's final wish came in 1955 when we were World Series Champs. My dad died shortly after', Wolfe said.

"My first game I was fortunate to sit a half-dozen rows behind the dugout. My seat was the last in a row of 4 or 6 before the railing separated us from the next section. Across the railing as I walked in was a living Hollywood legend at that time, Gabby Hayes," recalls Branch B. Rickey.

"In my early years, I went to the games with either my dad or my aunt. During the week, because my father worked and didn't get home till late, I would leave early from my house and stand on line on the first base side. You see back then general admission was first come takes all and the seats directly behind first base was up for grabs as soon as the gate opened," Robert Smith said.

"My dad would come out of the subway underground on a dead run with me waiting on line. I had already bought the tickets and all we had to do was run like hell," Smith said. "Later on as I got older, my buddies and I went all the time and sat in the bleachers for free with 50 Elsie the cow ice cream covers. Everybody knew everyone in the bleachers. My best friend till this day was a hated Yankee fan. We would fight on a regular basis but remained friends all these years," Bob said. "People can say whatever they want about old ballparks but there will NEVER be another Ebbets Field. Back then players signed autographs and would say "hello" and wave. They made you feel like you were part of the team," Smith said.

Herb Rosenblum had his dad take him to his very first major league game. "It was a doubleheader against Philadelphia. We were seated out in left field…left center to be exact about ten rows up. In the first game, Jackie Robinson hit a homer to left field. The ball struck one of the steel uprights and flew right towards us. I was too small but my father leaped up and grabbed it with his bare hand and tucked it against his chest as you would a football," Rosenblum said. "He let me hold the ball and I examined it so closely and so intensely that I believe, with my eyes shut, I could have described every smudge, every bruise and every nick on that ball. To me, it was the most valuable thing in the world. "I walked on air for a week afterwards and even conducted tours into my house so my friends could see it and touch the ball', Herb added. Born in 1934, Jack Foley brought his two brothers Ray 8 and Gerald 6 to Ebbets Field after taking two subways. "It wasn't dangerous like it is now," he says. It cost us 50 cents to sit in the bleachers and we'd take about 30 lettuce, tomato and baloney sandwiches with us. Our mom would give us about $4 (which was a lot of money in those days) to spend. We'd get two orange drinks and spend the whole day there. We collected newspapers and made $1 for every 100 we collected during the war," Foley said. "We'd get to Ebbets about 10 and watch batting practice and get some autographs and talk to the players," he said. Back then, the Dodgers were part of your family. You'd see players on the street and many lived in the neighborhood," Foley recalls.

Charles Heffernan thought the peanuts were great at Ebbets Field. He recalls a group sitting near him. "I was about 11, when my dad took me there for a Sunday game against Milwaukee. We had good seats, just up from the visitor's dugout. Behind us was a group of four guys, whose "leader" was a loud (but not obnoxious) fellow named Chuck," Heffernan said. "In mid-game, it was his turn to go get dogs and beer for the group. When he returned after a long time, he sat down and noticed that the Braves had scored three runs in his absence. When he asked his buddies how they scored, one of them said. 'We're not going to tell you'. Chuck then let out a plaintiff wail, 'You mean I gotta buy the Daily News tomorrow to find out what happened at the game I was at'," Heffernan said. "My main recollection is coming into the stands and seeing the field for the first time (I must have been eight or nine years old during the summer of 1948 or '49). The amazing green of the grass! The brilliant white of the uniforms. Remember, the only place that I saw the field was in the newspapers and on black and white TV," Fred Harber said.

"We used to sneak in on the weekends about 8 am through one of the metal gates that they opened up to deliver ice," said Stan Roth. "We would then hide in the upper left field stands until they opened the gates for the paying people. Sometimes we would go downstairs for autographs and one of the park policemen, Jo Jo Moore (a real fat guy), would constantly chase us away," Roth added. Jack Skelly's father was a policeman "and he use to get PAL tickets to Ebbets Field. "I'd round up the guys and we'd jump the trolley on Nostrand Ave. and head to the junction (Nostrand and Flatbush) and change trolleys for the ride to Ebbets Field. These tickets were for seats in the left field bleachers. I remember them as being wooden seats, front and back and the seat portion would fold up I guess for cleaning," Skelly said. "When we wanted some action we would yell

'We want a hit s**t' and if the seat next to you was empty we'd slam down the seat on the last word to emphasize our desire," Skelly said.

Frank Demaria was "11or 12" and spent his summer days at a recreation program run by Greenpoint YMCA. "It was a week day and the Y was taking a group of us to Ebbets Field for an afternoon game. We got there early and watched the players practicing on the field. We were in right field, one level up and on the field below us, Roger Craig was loosening up," Demaria recalls. "We kept calling to him to throw us up a ball. Just when one of our counselors called us from behind and we turned our heads, Roger throws a ball up. The ball hit the kid standing next to me on the forehead. Roger saw what happened and had one of the ushers bring him down on the field," Demaria said. "We could see Roger walking the kid into the Dodger dugout. He came back just before the game time. He told us he got to meet the team and they all signed a ball for him. I kept thinking how close I was to being the kid in the dugout. A little bump on the head would have been a small price for a lifetime memory," Demaria said.

"As children, we didn't measure someone by whether they were white, black or hispanic. We measured them by whether they rooted for the Dodgers, Giants or Yankees," Jimmy Mueller said. "Yankee fans could be tolerated because the Yankees were in a different league but a Giant fan in Brooklyn was the lowest of the low!," he said.

Fred Nash recalls that in the 1940's, "Everyone smoked in those days and you could only get mustard on your hotdogs. There was a sign in right field –Abe Stark Clothes- Hit Sign Win Free Suit. Carl Furillo was the right fielder and I don't think anyone hit the sign on the fly while he was the right fielder," Nash said.

"There was a big Benrus clock on top of the scoreboard and the Schaefer score board was hand operated. I recall a player named Bama Rowell hit the clock and broke it and there was a lot of confusion with the umpires because there wasn't any ground rules established at the time (to cover the situation)," Nash said.

"The Schaefer score board had a screen on top of it and there were a few holes in it from hard hit balls. Believe it or not, a Dodger by the name of Dixie Walker hit a line drive that went through one of those holes and a terrible argument followed because the opposing team claimed it couldn't be ruled a home run, " Nash said.

"There was a Dodger named Cookie Lavagetto who hit an umpire over the head during a game (that I attended) after being called out on a third strike. During that same game, the Dodger manager Leo Durocher had a fist fight with one of the security guards," Nash said.

Bob Gottdenker recalls "a man named Jack Pierce had a season box seat near third base and was a big fan of Harry 'Cookie' Lavagetto the third baseman of the Dodgers. Every Lavagetto at bat, he would scream 'Cookie' and release a balloon," Gottdenker said.

"My father took me to a game on June 30, 1955 a storied year in Brooklyn Dodger history. We had box seats on the third base side behind the dugout," Dennis Desmond recalled. Don Newcombe fouled a ball back, my dad caught it and our box seat neighbor Ezio Pinza ('Some Enchanted Evening' and South Pacific star) autographed it for us. I still have that ball," Desmond said.

Gerry O'Shea went to Ebbets Field with his 7th grade Parochial school class in 1951 when the Dodgers were playing the Boston Braves. "We get there early with seats in the left field bleachers and the Braves are taking batting practice. Shagging flies is their top pitcher and All Star lefty, Warren Spahn. We're standing at the rail, yelling out things like "Braves stink, yea Dodgers" nothing out of hand as the priest accompanying us is sitting about 3 rows from the rail. Mr. Spahn takes a walk over to the rail, looks up at the 11 and 12 year olds and says loud and clear, "Shut the F**k up, you little C**ksuckers". Dead silence and the priest finally says, "let's go boys, let's take our seats. A real sweetheart, Mr. Spahn," O'Shea adds.

Henry Becker was six years old "when I went to Ebbets Field for the first time in 1953. My first remembrance is emerging from the upper deck portal behind home plate to see the greatest expanse of green you could imagine". Becker also recalled "sitting in the upper deck behind home plate and being able to watch the starting pitchers warm up directly below throwing toward the backstop."

Mille Ducker was about 13 when she first went to see the Dodgers play. "I remember being so happy when I was old enough to take the Franklin Ave trolley to Ebbets Field with a friend or my sister." She also went to Ladies Day games where she sat "high up in the bleachers." "We got in for only .25 cents and had the time of our young lives rooting for Duke, PeeWee and Carl. We even had money left over for hotdogs and of course the yearbook (One of which I still have)," she said. Ducker also planned to play hooky on Ladies Day on "beautiful spring days in April and May" with eight of her friends in high school but there was a catch. "We all went to McAuley High School in Flatbush and wore the same uniforms and just feared that it was so obvious and that we would be caught," so they never really played hooky "but it was fun planning it anyway," Ducker said.

Proud Brooklyn fan

"My singular recollection of Ebbets Field was sneaking into it through a broken slat in the backfield. As I recall, it was a well known across Brooklyn kiddom that if you snuck in that way, the guards would look the other way…as long as you were a kid," said Bill Pasternak.

"I remember going to Ebbets Field as a kid with my brother on the IRT to Franklin Ave. running down all the way to the field and lining up for the bleachers for .60 cents…first come, first serve," Jerry Feldberg said. "When the gates opened, my brother and I ran all the way up the ramps to try to be the first ones in the bleachers in order to get the 'box seats' there. "We started with about three dollars each, this included subway fare, ticket to the game and food. We always got there first and left last, walking back to the subway talking about the game…either happy that we won or really down if we lost," Feldberg said. "That was in the early 1950's. As we got older, we bought real 'box seats' for $3 at first and I think they were up to $4.50 at the time the Dodgers moved to Los Angeles. Those were among the happiest days of my life, until the black day that we found we were losing OUR team," Feldberg said.

Alfred Albertus has a story about climbing into Ebbets Field over gates 13 and 14. "My friend, Edward Decker, was a very daring climber. He climbed the left field wall and somehow climbed over the extended spikes to prevent such a climb. "When the Green Coats 'ushers' appeared to grab him as he entered the field, he retreated to the spikes and sat on top of them until they went away," Albertus said. "His photo appeared on the back page of the NY Daily Mirror the next day," Alfred said. Another time, Sept 8, 1941 on a sold out day, Alfred and Edward improvised for seats. A photo was taken of them by a newspaper photographer because "we had been sitting on a steel girder supporting the ramp to the upper tier, in back of first base since there were no seats available," Albertus said.

Robert Lerner started going to Ebbets Field in 1942 with his dad until they left New York. "Brooklyn Dodger fans were real baseball fans. They understood the game, knew the players and came out to the game to enjoy themselves. They never had to be told when to cheer for the team, applauded good plays on both sides, did not have to be given a gift to go to the game and booed a players who did not give his all," Lerner said. "If you sat in the lower sections, near first base and third base, you could hear the players sometimes. When you sat in the bleachers, you had Hilda with her cow bell in the only reserved seat in the bleachers. You had gambling going on (what each pitch was going to be a ball or strike), arguments over who was a better ballplayer and 'who let that Giant fan in'. It was all done in fun," Lerner said.

Grace Lichtenstein used to collect baseball cards and autographs instead of dolls. "We never called them the boys of summer. But during the late 40's and early 50's, I was in my years of pre-teen innocence, and the Dodgers were practically gods in our Crown Heights household. Baseball was my family's religion, the Dodgers were our denomination, Ebbets Field was the church. We lived on Carroll Street near Franklin Avenue, a short walk from the ballpark" Lichtenstein says. "Some families celebrated a child's rite of passage with a communion or a bar mitzvah; my family commemorated my first time at an actual game. My grandfather, a native New Yorker whose encyclopedic knowledge of the team went back to the days of Wee Willie Keeler, accompanied me to left field lower deck seats at Ebbets Field. My father recorded the event in black and white on our 8-millimeter home movie camera. I still have that film, now on video, the year was 1948, and you can see manager Leo Durocher in the third base coach's box," Lichtenstein adds. Jim McElroy was not a Dodger fan but he still went to Ebbets Field. "I have been a Yankee fan since da day I entered this world, but I lived within walking distance of Charlie Ebbets' ball park and on occasion I would go with a couple of friends to see da dreaded Brooklyns play the game," he said. "This one particular game I am sitting in da left field seats about 15 feet on da fair side of da fair pole in da first row. Campy is up and hits one right at me (which I handled like all good catchers do). I was gonna throw it back on the field but all my buddies jumped me and said 'what are you crazy'. Ok, I kept it," McElroy admitted.

Bill Boggs remembers "in 1954. I was invited to Ebbets Field to try out for the Dodgers and play on their barnstorming team called 'Dodger Rookies'." "I was a pretty fair high school pitcher and the Dodgers had Al Campanis and one of their relief pitchers, Ben Wade talk to me. I was sent out to the Dodger bullpen in right field to warm up when Campanis and Wade came out and asked if I was ready," Boggs said.

"Ok," Wade says, "Let's see your fastball". I threw that ball so hard my groin still hurts…then I heard the death knell of my baseball career…'DON'T HOLD BACK SON…LET IT RIP'."

"As a 12 year old, Dodger pitcher Hugh Casey told my coach, 'I never saw a 12 year old throw that hard. My problem was at 17, I was still throwing hard for a 12 year old," Boggs said.

Morton Lapayover had his favorite place at Ebbets Field. It was the box seats in the bleachers. "You had to get there early, but there was one box that was in a straight line-the box, second base and home plate. You could see the break of a curve ball from there. And the highest price I remember for the regular season was 60 cents. It went to 90 cents for the World Series and we had to sleep outside overnight to get those seats but it was worth it," Lapayover said.

George Colligan witnessed first hand a conversion of a skeptic to a die hard Dodger fan many years ago. "Dot Neilis, a long time resident of Brooklyn and a highly respected Manhattan attorney, thought that baseball and the Dodgers (in particular) was something for the amusement of the rabble," said Colligan.

"One evening at dinner, as she was ranting about how awful it was that people wasted their time and money hanging around Ebbets Field, my father challenged her to attend a game. 'Of course, I'll go', she said (in that kind of 'I'll show you' way she had. So my father bought some tickets and off they went, my parents and Dot.

The story ends, of course, with Dot Neilis having lifetime season tickets to every Dodger home game AND her own night in Ebbets Field accompanied by the Dodger Symphoney," said Colligan. No one was more desolate, and no one called Walter O'Malley more terrible things, when the Dodgers left Brooklyn than the prominent and highly respected N.Y. Attorney Ms. Dorothy Neilis," Colligan explained. Alan Greenberg remembers the atmosphere at Ebbets Field. "The smell of beer… Schaefer was a sponsor. The vendors came around and they opened the cans with a can opener and poured the beer at your seat. And smoke everywhere, Lucky Strike was another sponsor. Then there were the dirty water hotdogs (boiled hot dogs). The bathrooms didn't smell so great either…old plumbing, concrete walls- a real institutional look," noted Greenberg.

Robert Gruber recalls that "under the stands there was an open runway for the players between the clubhouses and the dugouts. Many times I would thrust a pencil and paper through the bars and my Uncle Larry would shout 'Leo, sign it for the kid'. The field was incredibly green and we were so close we could hear every word of the infield chatter." Gruber also had an encounter with a legendary Dodger fan. "One sweltering day in the bleachers, Hilda Chester (with her ever present cowbell) wouldn't let us kids take our shirts off because of the threat of sunburn. Hilda Chester…my first dermatologist!" said Gruber. "I saw Hilda Chester many times. She always wore a hat, usually a dark coat, no make-up and always had the cowbell," said Bob Gottdenker. "Ebbets Field may have been small, but it had more love in it than any other major league park. I remember people like Hilda Chester (Cowbell Annie) with that string of pearls wrapped tightly around her neck, the Brooklyn Symphony band played 3 blind mice when an umpire made a bad call and buying peanuts outside the park because they were five cents cheaper," Jimmy a fan from Bushwick said. "I was there on Gil Hodges night when they gave him a brand new Pontiac. Although we didn't know these people on a personal level, it sure felt personal. I remember how bad I felt when Campy was in that accident and how betrayed I felt at the end of the season in 1957," he said.

Chapter 7   More Than a Ballpark

There were many other events at Ebbets Field that took place in the 57 years of it's existence beside major league baseball. College football, high school baseball and football, church services, boxing, negro league baseball, circuses, fund raisers and political rallies are just a few of the events held there.

One of the odder events transformed Ebbets Field into a giant movie house. Marcus Loew arranged with Ebbets in 1914 to use Ebbets Field for the showing of Thomas Ince's six reel The Wrath of the Gods. After more than 21,000 people paid their way into the park to see the film and accompanying live show, Loew began buying up the theatres that were to bear his name for decades. "Ebbets got half the proceeds from the Ebbets Field showing," according to Donald Dewey and Nicholas Acocella in their book The Ball Clubs. Ebbets Field also played a part in the Malbone Street Wreck that saw 97 people killed and over 100 hurt on November 1, 1918. Charles Ebbets Jr. was waiting for his father at Ebbets Field at the time of the accident and thought his father was on the train. After a frantic hour on the phone, Charles Jr. learned his father had been giving a speech for the War Savings Stamp campaign. After learning this, he opened Ebbets Field as a triage center so fifty of the less seriously injured rail passengers could be attended to by volunteer physicians.

Paul Robeson led Rutgers to a 14-0 victory over the Newport Naval Reserves Team on November 24, 1917 before 12,000 fans at Ebbets Field. The collection of former, college football stars were heavily favored over Rutgers. The New York Times reported that "the Newport sailors saw stars and roman candles after the stunning shock, and went down in defeat …in one of the most surprising games of a topsy-turvy gridiron season". At halftime, Rutgers students paraded around the turf and sang "On the Banks of the Old Raritan." The song "echoed through Flatbush and old Rutgers graduates hugged themselves and each other in glee and laughed at the perils of pneumonia as they took off their hats and

Notre Dame's 4 Horsemen 1923

threw them into the air," according to the Times. The students then formed a human letter "R" and left the field. Future actor, singer and black activist Paul Robeson played left end and was instrumental in scoring the second and final touchdown for Rutgers that day. "Quarterback Whitehill dropped back and took the ball on a long pass from the center, while Robeson in the meantime had rushed through the Newport players and was waiting just at the goal line. He reached up and grasped the ball as the naval men were upon him and all went down in a great heap. When the pile of players was unraveled, the ball was about 6 inches from the goal line but the officials ruled that the ball had gone over and Rutgers got another touchdown," noted the N.Y. Times.

In the Olympic year of 1920, a track meet was held at Ebbets Field. University of California sprinter Charlie Paddock won a 100 yard dash over his closest rival Jackson Scholz. Paddock, who was to become the "World's Fastest Human" later that year in Antwerp, had an unusual style of running that seemed awkward and stiff. He could run like a streak and had a habit of lunging at the finish line. He won three medals in Antwerp.

Another spectacular gala affair at Ebbets involved the "Fighting Irish" football team. The Notre Dame –Army game was switched from Cullum Hall Field in Hudson River Valley in 1923 to Ebbets Field because more seats were needed to accommodate fans. The World Series between the New York Yankees and New York Giants was played at the Polo Grounds and so that venue was unavailable that Saturday. It was a warm and pleasant October 13 when Notre Dame played Army in front of 30,000 plus fans at Ebbets Field. Another 10,000 people were turned away in what turned out to be the first sold out Notre Dame game that year. The Irish received one- third of the net receipts (over $19,000) for their trouble.

Bishop Laughton's Ed Clancy pitches in city championship game 1955

This was also the first game that the four horsemen, Elmer Layden, Don Miller, Jim Crowley and Harry Stuhldreher started together. It wasn't until a year later that Grantland Rice immortalized them in a game summary for the Herald Tribune. However, he noted to a friend "Brink" Thorne on the Ebbets Field sidelines in 1923 after almost being trampled on an end sweep that "it's worse than a cavalry charge…they're like a wild horse stampede."

Notre Dame shutout Army that day 13-0 and so dominated the cadets that they ended up ridiculing them by asking if their uniform stripes denoted how many years they were in college football before they enlisted.

In 1926, the most prolific goal scorer in US soccer history tallied four times in a 6-1 win over Canada at Ebbets Field. Archibald "Archie" Stark had 300 goals in his career and ranks 43rd on the all time list of world's top division scorers.

For many years, the circus would often parade past Borough Hall and then settle for a stay at Ebbets Field.

"I went to the Cole Bros. Circus at Ebbets Field with St Giles Hospital," Marie Cassidy Greening recalled. "Since my name was Cassidy, Hoppy (Hopalong Cassidy) was my favorite cowboy. He came to the hospital to visit us," she said. William Boyd (Hopalong Cassidy) toured with the Cole Bros. Circus in 1950. Children were admitted for half price except on Saturday and Sunday as tickets ranged from $3 to $1.

"I remember the rodeo at Ebbets too. Seems to me, the view was great there compared to the Garden (Madison Square)." said Marie Cassidy Greening Brooklyn Historian Ron Schweiger also went to the circus as a child of six or seven in the early fifties "I remember someone being shot out of a canon from down the right field line near the Dodger bullpen. He landed in a net that was at second base," Schweiger said.

Ivan Danzig, son of famous photographer Robert Olen, recalls Hopalong Cassidy coming to Ebbets Field. "I remember him on his gallant and majestic white horse Topper trotting around the field. All the kids were cheering and screaming. There was also a machine on the field launching candy bars to us in the stands".

M. Monroe waving at soccer game 1957

Fan John Crawford Nichols saw a famous personality at Ebbets Field. "At a Public High School championship baseball game, I saw Mayor Jimmy Walker throw out the first ball. He was late as usual and took forever to heave out the first ball but was charming. If he had taken much longer it would have been dark and Ebbets Field did not have lights yet," Nichols said with a chuckle. Nichols also attended professional football games at Ebbets Field. "The football Dodgers always had a good first team but reserves were not up to par. Guys like Pug Manders, Ace Parker and the Kinard brothers plus tight ends like Perry Schwartz were excellent," Nichols said. "I was sitting in the upper left field stands during one game. The Dodgers all keyed on a guy called Whizzer White and a QB and running back named Chuck Bond ran wild. You know what White became (Supreme Court Justice)," Nichols added. In 1942, the former Brooklyn Boys High football star Hal McCullough played one season, I could see he was not good enough for the pros," Nichols noted.

On October 21, 1944, President Franklin Roosevelt spoke before 16,000 people at a campaign rally at Ebbets Field for Senator Robert F. Wagner of New York. Ebbets Field was the first stop on a four borough swing by the president who spoke bareheaded and wore a big navy cape in a rainstorm caused by an Atlantic Ocean hurricane. Ten thousand policemen lined a motorcade route that included a flag-draped 50 car procession that lasted four hours through streets lined three deep with admirers on each side. Although the baseball season was over, Roosevelt did say, "I have never been to Ebbets Field before, but I have rooted for the Dodgers. I hope to come back here some day and see them play." FDR was hatless in a driving rain while he implored Brooklynites to vote "my old friend Bob." His tour was prompted by rumors of ill health and he traveled 51 miles in an open car to help dispel those rumors and have as many New Yorkers see him while campaigning.

Besides political fights, many World Championship fights were held at Ebbets Field. Filipino flyweight Poncho Villa knocked down Johnny Buff three times in the tenth round in route to a technical knockout in the 11th round during a September 14th, 1922 bout. Villa won the 112 pound title when Buff's seconds threw in the towel after 27 seconds of the 11th round in the first title fight held at Ebbets Field.

One Light Heavyweight Division fight was held on July 16, 1926 when Jack Delaney went 15 rounds against champion Paul Berlenbach. It was the third fight between the two fighters and Berlenbach had a 12 lb advantage over Delaney. Delaney, who fractured a bone in his left thumb in the third round, built an early lead on points. Berlenbach came back in the middle rounds to even the match but Delaney came back and won in the last five rounds with a furious attack in front of 46,000 fans that jammed Ebbets Field and paid $420,000 at the gate. Mickey Walker, billed as the Toy Bulldog, spotted Jack Sharkey 29 pounds and held him to a 15 round draw in a heavyweight fight to benefit the Free Milk Fund for Babies Inc.on July 22, 1931. Both fighters were upset with the decision. Sharkey, who cut Walker over the left eye and knocked him down in the fifth round, was a 3-1 favorite going into the fight. The decision drew cheers and boos from the Ebbets Field crowd of 32,000. They were clearly on the underdog's side from the beginning of the brawl until the end. Former heavy weight champ Gene Tunny thought Walker won while chairman of the New York boxing commission James Farley believed Sharkey won hands down. The fight box office was $210.000 and the crowd saw Sharkey warned three times for either low blows or head butting. Many thought Sharkey gave a lackadaisical performance while the undersized Walker gave him all he could handle and more. Sharkey, who was being considered for a championship fight with Max Schemling, came on strong in the closing rounds but couldn't finished off Walker.

Circus at Ebbets Field

Another Light-Heavyweight Championship occurred on Aug 5, 1931 as Maxie Rosenbloom beat Jimmy Slattery in fifteen rounds in front of a disappointing 10,000 fans. The fight billed as the Battle of The Playboys was a far from an impressive affair. Slattery tried to rally in the 13th round and did cut Rosenbloom on the chin but it was too little too late as he lost on points for the second straight time. It was a lopsided fight with Slattery only winning one round. He had previously beaten Rosenbloom in four out of six fights. Rosenbloom constantly kept him off balance with short jabs and a left hand that he couldn't seem to avoid all night. The Depession Era gate of $35,000 was one of the lowest in New York in years. Rosenbloom had such an easy time with the Buffalo Irishman that he hopped out of the ring after the fight and kept an engagement on Broadway. Gus Lesnevich gave rotund Tami Mauriello an 18 1/2 pound advantage in their July 30, 1947 light-heavy weight bout. .Lesnevich won a non-title 10 round decision before 25,000 fans at Ebbets Field. The gate was estimated at $125,000 for the Damon Runyon Cancer Fund fight. Before the fight, the acting director of Madison Square Garden Sol Strausss said the winner would get a non-title shot at Joe Louis in November if his performance was impressive.Lesnevich,

Clowning at Ebbets

who had previously beaten Mauriello in August and November of 1941, was tattooing Mauriello regularly with punches for seven rounds and almost took him out three times before getting rocked with a right hand in the eight round. He held on for the next two rounds for a lack luster upset victory in one of the last big fights at Ebbets Field.

High school football had a prominent place at Ebbets Field in the off season. "For an number of years, Brooklyn Prep and St. John's Prep played a Thanksgiving Day football game at Ebbets Field," according to Bernie McCoy. "It was preceded the night before by a "gala" at Brooklyn Prep. This event was most frequently called a "racket" but went by several other labels, most notably "A Social and Athletic Gathering" (it stayed relatively social until about 11 and then the athletics started). The end of the evening was usually signaled by the arrival of representative from the local precinct," said McCoy. "The celebrants would then adjourn to nearby Snyders where several subsequent rounds (in several interpretations of the word) would commence. This would be followed by the breakfast course at a local diner then an early morning trek to Ebbets for the 10 am kickoff.

"Not surprisingly, Brooklyn Prep, St John Prep nor Ebbets Field never made a great effort to publicize this annual bacchanalia, but there is enough material surrounding this gridiron clash for a book in itself," McCoy recalled.

"On Thanksgiving Day in the early 50's, Brooklyn Prep and St. John's Prep met in the traditional game at Ebbets Field at 10am. Try as we might, in order not to ruin our appetites for a great turkey dinner, we could not resist a frank or two from the concession stands...plus a hot chocolate (which quickly turned cold on those chilly November mornings," Tony Sogluizzo recalls. "They would get crowds in the 20,000 plus vicinity. I also remember seeing Brooklyn Prep play Fordham Prep under the lights there (a 6-6 tie in 1952)." Said Tony Sogluizzo Jerry Feldberg attended football games at Ebbets Field . "I think we ate the same kind of things as at the baseball games and I know it was colder than a witches t*t on Halloween. We had blankets to keep warm and I do remember fires in big pickle barrels that people hovered around. There were chestnut vendors outside. That much I am positive of since I loved them and took them in with me," said Feldberg.

Jack (Popeye) Doyle went to a church at Ebbets Field. "Back in the thirties there was a Holy Name Sunday that used to encompass all the Holy Name Societies of all the parishes in Brooklyn. The members of the Holy Name Society "marched along Flatbush Avenue, they were going north to the south and south to the north and when they met at Empire Blvd. They turned and went the two blocks down Empire Blvd. to Ebbets Field. The men and their sons entered Ebbets Field at that point," said Doyle. "And their families (the mothers and daughters and small sons) would go to Ebbets Field. It was open for them for the whole day. I belonged to the Holy Cross choir that was well known at the time in the area. The Holy Cross Choir was chosen to do the Benediction. The organ was set up back of second base and Gladys Goodding was playing the organ and we did the Benediction," Doyle said. "The men met their families in the stands and by the time you had all those people getting together there was about 18-20,000 people in Ebbets Field. I was chosen to do the solo for the Panis Angelicus at the Benediction. I was seven years old," Doyle remembers.Jack "Popeye" Doyle, by the way, later joined the New York police department and was a composite character portrayed by Gene Hackman in his Oscar winning performance in the French Connection. He recently celebrated his 50th wedding anniversary.

Tony Soluizzo was another Dodger fan who participated in the services held at Ebbets Field. "I would say it was about 50 or so years ago that our contingent of altar boys from Our Lady of Refuge Parish (sponsoring parish for that year's Knights of Columbus Rally and Mass at Ebbets Field) had the privilege of sitting both in the Dodger dugout (and clubhouse) during that rainy Sunday afternoon. "We had marched in procession from the church (at Foster and Ocean Ave.) to Ebbets Field," he said. "It was a thrill to be in the inner sanctum of our heroes…and even though it was pouring rain all afternoon… we were in Dodger Blue Heaven. The Dodger clubhouse was small and cramped compared to today's spacious facilities but this was indeed sacred ground to us! What a thrill seeing the lockers of Reese, Robby, Furillo, Gil, Campy, the Duke, Cox, Newk, Erskine, Roe, Labine, etc." Sogluizzo said. "Pee Wee Reese, Gil Hodges, Spider Jorgenson and Dick Whitman all shared an apartment across the street from Our Lady of Refuge in those days…we were lucky enough to get their autographs one day," he said.

Dennis Desmond had mixed feelings when attending the church service at Ebbets Field. "All the parishes in Brooklyn marched and most had large groups. We marched from IHM (Immaculate Heart of Mary) and met neighboring parishes along the march," he said. A neighbor who used to chase us all the time from playing Chinese handball on the side wall of his house marched with Holy Innocents. "He was always angry at our handball, or punchball or stickball games but when he saw us at the Holy Name Rally, all was forgiven," Desmond said. "My friend and I always gave him the biggest hello and enthusiastic smiles and he always returned the greeting. But it only happened at the Rally. The rest of the year it was 'go on, get out of here'. We went along Prospect Park by the Parade Grounds and ended at the great ball field with parishes coming up all ways from McKeever, Sullivan, Bedford Ave. and marching through the gate in center field right by the 401' mark. Then we sat in the stands and the service was held. I'm not sure, I think it was a mass and maybe a benediction. Then we all processed out," Desmond said. "I did feel funny not seeing Duke Snider in centerfield as we came through the gate and have to admit my mind wandered during the mass as I looked out on the altar. Sometimes thinking about Pee Wee, Gil, and Carl Furillo, Campy etc instead of the homily. But when you're a kid, those things happened especially to kids from Brooklyn," Dennis Desmond remembered. "Dodger souvenirs were on display as you were arriving and leaving so that could also distract a die hard fan," he added. Stan Field saw many football games at Ebbets Field during the 40's and 50's. "The traditional game between Tilden and Jefferson was played At Ebbets Field when I was a youngster. By the time I was a student at Tilden (1950-1953), the game had been moved to another field," he said.

"During World War II, there were army base games played there. To get in, you had to buy a war bond. I can vaguely remember seeing Fort Mitchell play another army team. The Brooklyn Dodgers of the old American Football League (circa 40's to very early 50's) played there and I can remember going to a game to see them play the New York Yankees (who later became the Boston Yankees in that league). Needless to say, the league didn't last very long," Field said.

According to Ed Donovan the Dodgers were good to Brooklyn high schools. "Every spring some high school teams played a game at Ebbets Field when the Dodgers were on the road. I played for

FDR at Ebbets

Eastern District High School and in the spring of 1953 we played Bushwick High School at Ebbets," said Donovan. "Playing a game at Ebbets Field produced a lot of adrenaline. I remember walking around the infield and thinking that it's impossible to make an error. We were not used to playing on diamonds that were so well maintained," said Donovan. "Our team used the Dodger dugout (first base side) and that was a kick as we imagined that we were sitting where Gil and Campy sat, etc. Because the field was small in comparison to other big league parks, we all probably tried to hit one out. Of course, that's a mistake. My parents did not get to see me play too many high school games as they both employed, but they made a point of being there for this particular game against Bushwick High School," Donovan said.

In 1955, Ed Clancy pitched for Bishop Loughlin High School in the semi finals for the city championship at Ebbets Field. "Pitching a game at Ebbets Field was a childhood fantasy come to life. I remember watching Happy Felton's Knothole Gang on TV and wishing that I could have the opportunity to meet a real live Brooklyn Dodger and sit in the dugout with them during the game." Clancy said. "Walking down the ramp and seeing that beautiful field of perfect green grass and the familiar signs around the outfield walls was truly a Kodak moment.

"When I threw that first warm up pitch, I had no feeling in my arm. My legs felt like jello and my mouth was so dry, I could not even spit. "How nervous was I? "On a scale of 1 to 10, I maxed out. After facing the first batter, I was fine." Clancy eventually pitched in all three New York parks (including the

Polo Grounds and Yankee Stadium) and signed a minor league contract with the Philadelphia Phillies organization but had his budding career come to an end with a fall from a horse.

Andy Kovacs remembers "It was a practice of the Brooklyn Dodgers management to make the field available to the local high school teams when the Dodgers were out of town. "Such an opportunity came while I was in my last year at Bushwick High School. It was the Spring of 1953, I was the school photographer and was afforded the opportunity to travel to Ebbets Field with the team," Kovacs said. "I sat in the home team's dugout, what a thrill for this sixteen year old. I discovered why the players stood up and walked to the field when a ball was hit to left field. You could not see the left field wall while you sat in the dugout. It wasn't even close…the infield rose from the first baseline and completely hid the wall," Kovacs said. "To this day, I have no idea if this was common practice or something peculiar to Ebbets. It may have provided drainage," Kovacs noted.

On May 12, 1957, the Israeli Hapoel soccer team played a select All Star American team in an International game at Ebbets Field. Judge Samuel Leibowitz previously cabled the Israeli team and asked them what American they would most like to meet. "As athletes, we'd like to meet the Brooklyn Dodgers: as men, Marilyn Monroe," they replied. Marilyn Monroe thus became the official mascot of the Israeli team and kicked out the first ball at Ebbets Field. Sammy Davis also attended the game. The Israeli Hopoel defeated the All Star team 6-4 in front of 30,000 fans at Ebbets Field The game was part of the Salute to Israel Festival and the beginning of a good-will tour.

Chapter 8   Wait Till Next Year - Winning and Heartbreaks

When the 1948 season began, Durocher was back from exile in California and the roster was cleansed of Eddie Stanky and Dixie Walker. Jackie Robinson came to spring camp out of shape after being feted the whole off season for his remarkable accomplishment of integrating baseball and helping lead the Dodgers to the pennant. Durocher was not pleased.

Durocher constantly reminded folks that Burt Shotten had won the pennant with "his team" and was not endearing himself with the front office with his caustic nature. Stanky was shipped off to the Boston Braves in a salary dispute and that opened the door for Jackie Robinson to move to second base, In turn, Gil Hodges moved over to first base making room for Roy Campanella to be promoted to catcher from the minors.

Pee Wee Reese was a standard at short and slick fielding Billy Cox was at third base after coming over in the Dixie Walker trade with the Pirates. Walker had previously been offered the manager's job at St. Paul in the American Association but turned it down. Duke Snider was installed in center and Carl Furillo shifted over to right field where he was incredible with his uncanny ability to play caroms off the 20 ft right field wall and 20ft fence on top of it. Left field was up for grabs. Preacher Roe had also come over in the Walker trade and he became a prominent member of the pitching staff along with Ralph Branca, Erv Palica, Jack Banta and Rex Barney.

The 1948 season was a transitional one for the Dodgers. Towards the end of May, the club was floundering. Durocher seemed to be walking on egg shells and wasn't his usual self. He almost seemed timid in his dealing with umpires. By July 5th the team hit rock bottom when the Giants scored three ninth inning runs to defeat them 6-4 in front of over 33,000 fans at Ebbets Field. Durocher tried to stop a five game losing streak by inserting three catchers into the lineup along with rookie outfielder George Shuba but they couldn't avoid landing in last place. The regular catcher Bruce Edwards played third base, Gil Hodges played first and Roy Campanella (who was called up that week from St. Paul in the American Association) was the catcher and had three hits and scored twice but it wasn't enough.

The Dodgers were a stagnant squad and going nowhere when Rickey decided to shake up the team in a big way. Giant's owner Horace Stoneham had asked Rickey for permission to hire Burt Shotten to replace his manager Mel Ott. Branch Rickey suggested Stoneham might prefer Durocher instead.

Branch Rickey met with Durocher in his office and mentioned the Giants were interested in his services. Leo took the hint and packed his bags and moved across the bridge to Harlem and the Polo Grounds. Dodger fans took it in stride but Giant fans felt flummoxed. The guy they loved to hate was in charge of their team now. Burt Shotten replaced Durocher once again and the Dodgers picked up steam to finish in third place just seven and a half games behind the Boston Braves.

In 1949 the Dodgers were on a mission. From the first day of spring training, when Branch Rickey converted a former naval air base in Vero Beach, Florida into a baseball college until the last day of the season, the Dodgers were maturing into a powerhouse ball club.

Don Newcombe arrived in May and with his 17-8 record became the first black star pitcher. Roy Campanella hit 22 homers and solidified the catcher position in his first full season. Jackie Robinson rebounded from an off season and was the National League's most valuable player. He lead the league with a .342 average, knocking in 124 runs and he stole a league high 37 bases.

Half way through the 1949 season, the All Star game (16th) was played at Ebbets Field for the first and only time . On that July 12th, four black ballplayers were on the field for the first time in All Star history. Larry Doby of the Cleveland Indians joined Newcombe, Campanella and Robinson in baseball's mid summer showcase. Many of the 32,577 fans got wet during two rain showers (one of which lasted 13 minutes) and went home early. The game raised almost $80,000 for the player's pension fund.

Joe DiMaggio was chosen as a reserve and was the star of the game with a single, double and three runs batted in to lead the American League to an 11-7 victory in front of fans who saw the Junior Circuit win for the 12th time in 16 tries. The American League squad scored four runs off Newcombe in the first inning and was on their way to victory. The National League had Stan Musial and Ralph Kiner hit homeruns but it couldn't make up for their squad's five errors and 13 hits the American League produced. The sloppily played game caused many to call for an end to the affair. Branch Rickey, for one, wanted to see an end to the managers been stuck with playing the fan's selections for the first three innings. "The manager should not be forced to start with the fan's top selections –and play them for three innings," Rickey said. He favored the manager playing whomever he wanted for best effect. Rickey felt having a set lineup to start a game tied a manager's hands.

After the All Star game, the Cardinals and Dodgers battled down to the final day of the season with the Brooklyn squad ahead by one game. It took an extra innings game but the Bums won 9-7 for their second pennant in three years.

A familiar face to the Brooklyn faithful, Casey Stengel, was now the manager of the New York Yankees. He was in his first year at the helm. The Yankees squeaked into first place on the last day of the season against Ted William's Boston Red Sox. The first two games of the 1949 World Series were shutouts. Allie Reynolds beat Don Newcombe after Tommy Henrich of the Yankees hit a Newcombe curveball into the right field stands for a 1-0 victory. Brooklyn got revenge the next day with Preacher Roe winning another 1-0 game over Vic Raschi when Gil Hodges drove in the only run with a second inning single. The Yankees took the next three games at Ebbets Field, 4-3, 6-4 and 10-6.

The 1950 Dodgers were favorites to repeat but Philadelphia Phillies "Whiz Kids" surprised them and just about everyone in baseball. With a furious comeback, the Dodgers pulled within two games of first place on the final weekend of the season. Their opponent that weekend at Ebbets Field was Philadelphia .The Dodgers took command and won the first game 7-3 for their ninth straight win. Don Newcombe faced Phillies ace Robin Roberts in the showdown game. With the Phillies ahead by a run, Pee Wee Reese lifted a fly ball into the right field screen about five feet inside the foul pole. The ball dropped to the top of the wall above the red, white and blue Esquire Boot Polish sign. Reese scampered around the bases for an inside the park homer run while Philly players looked on in dismay.

Dodger fan Barry Becher was at the final game with his friend Norm Schimmel. "I was at the last game of the 1950

Walter O'Malley and employee Lee Hill

season with Norm. We snuck in the late innings. We were both 9 years old. We were standing down the left field line right where Jim Konstanty (Phillie reliefer) was warming up. We saw Duke (Snider) drill a line drive single to center and (Richie) Ashburn throw out Cal Abrams at the plate," Becher said. The bases were loaded after Jackie Robinson was walked but the Phillies Robin Roberts got Carl Furillo and Gil Hodges out and the rally was over. "Then in the 10th, Dick Sisler hit an opposite field homerun into the first few rows in left and we went home really sad," said Becher The Phillies won 4-1. It was their first pennant since 1915.

On October 26, an even greater surprise took place when Branch Rickey resigned as President of the Brooklyn Dodgers just as his contract was to expire. Walter O'Malley had been making Rickey's life miserable. According to Harold Parrott who held a variety of positions with the Dodgers over the years, "Making jokes about Rickey was the main sport at Room 40 (at the Hotel Bossert where O'Malley gathered his buddies in their private eating and drinking place). O'Malley began to nitpick and deplore almost everything that went on in Rickey's office," Parrott said.

Rickey had a 25% share of the club and each partner (O'Malley, John L. Smith or Rickey) had an option to meet any bona fide offer that someone else might make to buy that partner's share. O'Malley and Smith's widow were afraid an outsider might pick up Rickey's share and join Steve McKeever's daughter Dearie and her husband Jim Mulvey in stalemating any decisions if they had half of the team shares. They also hoped to pick up Rickey's share cheap at the $350,000 he paid during the war. Pittsburgh Pirate owner Jim Galbreath talked New York real estate developer William Zeckendorf into offering $1.05 million for Rickey's share. Of course, Galbreath had designs on acquiring Rickey's services and one good turn deserved another. According to broadcaster Ernie Harwell, "He (Rickey) and O'Malley didn't get along and he got forced out. I know when they parted ways, he (Rickey) stuck it to O'Malley with the sale of the stock …that sort of thing. He got a lot of money. He was a good businessman." Walter Francis O'Malley swallowed hard and paid up. He also coughed up an extra $50,000 for Zeckendorf's trouble. Harold Parrott met Rickey outside the Bossert Hotel after the sale. "He was in tears, despite the million bucks in his pocket," Parrott said. "He did not want to leave this baseball juggernaut he had built, with all its fine, upcoming young stars," said Parrott.

O'Malley who graduated in 1926 from University of Pennsylvania, also earned a degree from Fordham Law School. He was the Bronx born son of a New York City commissioner of Public Markets. As a lawyer, O'Malley brought clients to Ebbets Field and eventually became a director in 1932. During World War II, he replaced Wendell Wilkie as the team's lawyer and bought into the club with partners Branch Rickey and John Smith.

Shortly after taking over in 1950, O'Malley fined any office worker one dollar for mentioning Rickey's name. It wasn't that he needed the money. His holdings included ownership of the New York Subway Advertising Company (estimated value $7 million), partnership in the Brooklyn Borough Gas Company, part owner of a $5 million building materials company and 6% ownership of the Long Island Railroad.

At 47 years of age, Walter O'Malley was in charge of the Dodgers and he quickly brought in his own people. Burt Shotten was fired and replaced by former Dodger coach Charlie Dressen as manager. Buzzy Bavasi and Fresco Thompson (originally hired by Larry MacPhail) were promoted. Bavasi was de facto general manager and Thompson ran the farm system. Perhaps it was just a coincidence or fate that occurred in 1950 when Giant owner Horace Stoneham persuaded Matty Schwab (the head grounds keeper at Ebbets Field) to switch allegiances and tend to his shabby playing field. Schwab had Stoneham build a two- bedroom apartment under the left field grandstand rent free for him and his family.

The next year in 1951, the Dodgers were more determined to capture the pennant flag and figured the Phillies were a one year fluke. By August 11, they were 13 ½ games ahead of the hated Giants and seemed ready to coast to their third pennant in five years but something strange happened. Although they kept winning, the Giants kept gaining ground. Early in the spring. a rookie named Willie Mays was brought up from the minors and gradually got acclimated to the majors. The Giants won 16 in a row and closed the gap to six games. At one point, the Giants won 36 out of 43 games to narrow the Dodger margin.

Leo Durocher led the Giants to a first place tie at the end of the season and a two out of three playoff series was scheduled. Durocher was bubbling with enthusiasm for his team. "They've been great …just great. "You just can't put your finger on any one guy and say that he did it. It has been a team job and each and every one of them is entitled to a gob of credit," Durocher said. "Everyone quit on them but they never quit on themselves. If there is any justice at all, they'll win it because they deserve it. I never in my life got such a bang out of baseball as I have this year," he said.

The Giants won the first game at Ebbets Field 3-1 and the playoff sifted to the Polo Grounds. Dodger pitcher Clem Labine shutout the home team 10-0 and it seemed fate was on the Brooklyn side after game two. However Labine now says, "It was one of the most forgotten games ever pitched" because of what happened the next day when "our enemy … Thompson hit that home run."

Don Newcombe held off the Giants through eight innings and left the mound with a 4-2 lead and two men on base in the ninth inning during the third and deciding game. Ralph Branca was summoned from the bullpen and his second pitch was deposited in the third row of the left field stands by Giant Bobby Thompson for the "Shot Heard Around The World." Final score Giants 5-4 over the Dodgers.

The Dodger's pennant dreams were crushed for the second year in a row. Dodger fans couldn't believe it. Grace Lichtenstein was one of those fans. "My girl scout troop was a Dodger's fan club, so it was only natural for us to huddle around a radio at our regular Wednesday afternoon meeting to hear the deciding game of the playoffs …," said Lichtenstein. "When Bobby Thompson hit his homer, he broke many hearts, but none more shatteringly than those 25 innocent little Brooklyn girls in uniforms who sat stunned, then began sobbing in a basement somewhere on Crown Street," Lichtenstein said. "I walked home in a daze. I can't remember if my parents tried to console me. Nothing in my short life had prepared me for such an event that was overwhelmingly awful, so inconceivable," recalled Lichtenstein.

In some apartment buildings civil wars almost broke out. Jimmy Mueller was in one of those apartments. "My dad was a rabid Dodger fan and my godfather was a rabid Giants fan. In 1951, when Bobby Thompson hit that homerun off of Branca, my godfather was screaming in the hallway of our apartment house, the same thing Russ Hodges (Giant announcer) was screaming 'The Giants Won the Pennant'. My dad then yelled down the stairs that if he didn't shut up, he was 'Gonna come down there and punch him in the nose'," said Mueller. They had been friends since they were kids. Bullpen coach Clyde Sukeforth was given his walking papers after the season. He had told manager Dressen that Carl Erskine was throwing his curves in the dirt while warming up next to Ralph Branca. After hearing that, Dressen had his mind made up to call on Branca for his date with destiny.

The season ending disaster was shrugged off the next year as the Dodgers beat out the Giants by four ½ games even though they lost ace Don Newcombe to the military as the Korean War raged. Rookie fireballer Joe Black emerged as a relief ace and led the team in victories with 15.

One of the more powerful displays of the Dodgers took place early in the '52 season and fans Norm Schimmel and Barry Becher were both there, Norm Schimmel remembers when Duke Snider's homerun highlighted a 15 run first inning of a 19-1 victory on May 22, 1952. "The opponent was Cincinnati…Blackwell pitched for them and Chris Van Cuyk for us," Schimmel said. "He (Van Cuyk) had to go warm up twice during the inning. Reese and Cox batted three times each in the first inning," Norm added. Barry Becher, who has become friends with Duke Snider, says Duke remembers the game too. "He batted three times, hit a home run, walked and was called out on strikes to end the inning. Dixie Howell, the catcher for Cincy, told Duke the next day that the ball was six feet outside," Becher said.

Besides the 15 runs, the Dodgers racked up 10 hits, seven walks and two hit batsmen during that famous inning.

Another memorable game occurred on June 20 when Carl Erskine no hit and shut out the Chicago Cubs 5-0. Carl Furillo, Andy Pafko and Roy Campanella hit home runs to help defeat the Cubs who were no hit for the first time in 47 years. Erskine, whose wife had promised they would go on a picnic if he pitched a no-hitter as he left the house earlier in the day, only threw 103 pitches before only 13,232 fans in a rain delayed game at Ebbets Field.

Helping Erskine's cause was the ground crew under Eddie Durham direction when they set a new record by getting down the nylon tarp in one minute and twenty seconds before the rain soaked the field. Erskine walked Cub pitcher Willie "the Knuck" Ramsdell on four pitches in the third inning for the only blemish in the game. "I was in a hurry to get the side out," Erskine said. "The rain was coming and I was anxious to hurry it up so it would be a legal game. I kept firing fast balls to Ramsdell and couldn't get one over," Erskine explained. Rain delayed the game for 44 minutes but Erskine still had his stuff and retired the rest of the Cub hitters even though he only struck out one batter (Dee Fondy in the 8th). Walter O'Malley sent champagne to the locker room and presented Erskine with a $500 bonus check for the shut out. It was the first Dodger no-hitter at Ebbets Field since 1946 when Ed Head no hit the Braves. While newcomer Joe Black mastered the relief work, another rookie, Billy Loes (a 22 yr old from Queens) a right handed curveballer won 13 games to offset Newcombe's loss.

The Yankees won the American League pennant from the Cleveland Indians by just two games. Mickey Mantle attained top billing with the Yankees, replacing Joe Dimaggio who retired after the '51 season. he led them to their fourth straight pennant but not before Carl Erskine helped lead the Dodgers to a 6-5 win in Game 5 after pitching eleven innings and retiring the last nineteen Yankees in a row.

In 1952, Bill Boggs was 15 years old and got to go to the World Series at Ebbets Field. "Our team had just won the Coney Island League Championship. It was to become a little more important later in life because to win, we had to beat a team called the Parkviews, four straight games. That was Sandy Koufax's team (of course Koufax wasn't KOUFAX then. Me and Tony Imperato got awards as co-MVPs that included tickets to Game 6 (of the 1952 World Series). It was ironic in that Tony and I were Yankee fans. We were in the left field stands surrounded by the Dodger faithful," Boggs said. The Dodgers returned to Brooklyn up three games to two, needing just one win to get their first World Series. "It was (Vic) Raschi against (Billy) Loes, a game made famous by Loes losing a ground ball in the sun. The Yankees won 3-2 and then won game 7 in another close contest," said Boggs

Mickey Mantle, the muscular blond switch hitting 20 year old was instrumental in winning Game 6 and 7 and surfaced as legitimate superstar of series play. His homerun in Game 6 evened the series and he drove in two runs in the 4-2 Yankee victory in Game 7. It was the fourth championship in a row for the Yankees and another bitter pill for the Brooklyn faithful and another "Wait Till Next Year" finish.

The 1953 Dodger team was a powerhouse ready to steam roll anyone that got in their way. Five of their starting players hit over .300 and they led the American and National League in six different categories (home runs, batting and slugging average, runs scored, stolen bases and fielding percentage). Carl Furillo won the batting championship with a .344 average although he had to sit out the last part of the season after getting injured in a fight. "Leo Durocher, when he was manager of the Giants, rode Furillo nuts until one day Carl charged into the Giant dugout and wrestled with Leo. In the scuffle someone stepped on Carl's hand and he broke it and missed the last few weeks of the season but he won the batting title," said fan Robert Lerner.

The pitching staff was led by Carl Erskine's 20-6 record. Russ Meyer won 15, Loes won 14 and Preacher Roe and Clem Labine each won 11 games. Many people consider the 1953 Dodger team the best Brooklyn ever had. They led the Braves by 13 games and sewed up the pennant on September 12 . Their 105 victories were the most in franchise history.

The 50th World Series had the Yanks and Dodgers tangle for the second year in a row. The Yankees led the American League in batting average and earned run average even though they only had two .300 hitters and no 20 game winner. New York skipper Casey Stengel employed his platoon system to perfection.

The first two games went to the Yanks 9-5 and 4-2 at Yankee Stadium. Back in Brooklyn, Carl Erskine set a World Series by striking out 14 Yankees in Game 3 and Roy Campanella hit a homerun with a broken finger to win the game 3-1. Jackie Robinson also contributed three hits as the largest Ebbets Field World Series crowd of 35,270 witnessed their beloved Bums hold off the Bronx Bombers. Among the rabid fans were visiting dignitaries like General Douglas MacArthur, Governor Thomas Dewey, Adlai Stevenson and movie star Susan Hayward.

In Game 4, the Dodgers jumped all over New York lefty Whitey Ford for three runs in the first inning and knocked him out of the game in the second inning. Duke Snider had a homer and two doubles and 1953 Rookie of the Year Junior Gilliam added three doubles to lead the Dodgers to a 7-3 victory to knot the series in front of 35,000 plus fans at Ebbets Field

Game Five was a slugfest with both teams contributing 25 hits and 47 total bases. The Yankees outlasted the Dodgers with Mickey Mantle producing a gland slam into the upper left field stands to top off an 11-7 win. The Dodgers Billy Cox and Junior Gilliam hit home runs but they were out powered by the Bombers who had Gene Woodling, Gil McDougald and Billy Martin contribute homers along with Mantle's crusher.

Game 6 saw Carl Furillo hit a dramatic, opposite field homerun to right field to tie the score in the top of the ninth inning at Yankee Stadium. However, the Bum's jubilation was short lived after Billy Martin's record tying twelfth Series hit knocked in the winning run in the Yankee ninth.

The Dodgers were becoming lovable losers. It was the seventh time they had lost a World Series and fourth time in seven years they had the Yankees beat them. They were beginning to look like the Greek legend of Sisyphus. He was punished and forced to roll a stone to the top of a hill but just before reaching it, the stone would roll to the bottom. He would then have to start all over again with a similar result. On the other hand, the Yankees had won their record five consecutive Championship and they seemed invincible. While Dodger fans were licking their wounds, Walter O'Malley surveyed the baseball landscape and didn't like what he saw.

The Boston Braves moved their franchise to Milwaukee in 1953. It was the first time in 50 years that baseball had moved a franchise and what a success it was. The Braves drew 1,826,397 in their new 43,000 seat County Stadium and came in second place to the Dodgers. The Milwaukee Braves outdrew the Dodgers by 650,000 fans and O'Malley grew alarmed. The Braves had a larger stadium, greater parking capacity (10,000 cars) and a blackout on all home games compared to the Dodgers. Brooklyn generally made more money than any other National League until now but O'Malley was afraid of being left behind. He prophesied that if this continued Milwaukee would be able to outbid the Dodgers for any new talent but he wasn't going to go down without a fight.

Early in 1952, O'Malley commissioned architect Norman Bel Geddes to design a domed stadium to replace Ebbets Field. The next year he sold Ebbets Field to Marvin Kratter, a real estate developer, and leased the park for five more years. O'Malley complained that he only had room to park 700 autos and that the neighborhood around Ebbets Field was becoming run down and that the park's seating capacity was too small.

Another off season jolt happened when manager Chuck Dressen was let go after winning two pennants in a row. Dressen asked for a three- year contract after the 1953 World Series. He figured that after winning 198 games in three years and being the first Brooklyn manager to win two straight pennants he deserved a little bit of security. Dressen's ailing, hospitalized wife even wrote O'Malley a letter demanding a three year contract but O'Malley noted that the Dodgers had "paid more managers not to manage than any club". Of course he was referring to Max Carey and Casey Stengel who were paid after being terminated in the middle of their contracts during the thirties.

O'Malley was offering Dressen a one year deal…take it or leave it. "Charley knows our proposition and the next move is strictly up to him," O'Malley said. Dressen stubbornly refused, "I felt if Eddie Stanky got a three year contract for finishing third in St. Louis and Leo Durocher two years for finishing fifth with the Giants, I deserved more than a one-year deal," he said.

Walter O'Malley wouldn't budge and Dressen was out and Walter Alston was in. Alston had been the Dodger minor league manager of the Montreal Royals but had never managed in the big leagues. Pee Wee Reese turned down the job and it was rumored that former Giant star and ex-manger Bill Terry was considered but O'Malley opted for a company man. Fans and many players wondered who Alston was.

Walter Alston was the strong, silent type who managed 13 years in the minors before getting his chance at the majors (his one at bat as a player was a strikeout in 1936). Branch Rickey got Alston his start managing in the Brooklyn system and by 1947 said, "Alston is the man we're grooming to manage the Dodgers someday." For his part, Alston felt he knew the Dodger players and was ready for the job. "I'd been in the minors a long time. I had managed 17 of the 25 players at one time or another in the past at Saint Paul or Montreal. I had the advantage of knowing what to expect of them," he said.

Another surprise came in the spring when broadcaster Red Barber abandoned Ebbets Field after 15 years in a salary dispute and decided to work for the Yankees instead of O'Malley. Native New Yorker Vin Scully took over and became a success.

The 1954 Dodgers slumped and came in second place. Don Newcombe was back from the army but only won nine games. Roy Campanella was injured most of the season and hit a disappointing .207. Bone chips in his hand plagued Campy most of the season. Other players injured included Jackie Robinson with a bruised heal, Billy Loes with a pulled muscle, Pitcher Russ Meyer missed ten days with a spiked shin, Pee Wee Reese had a bad leg, Johnny Podres had an appendectomy and Gil Hodges had a hemorrhoid problem. Robinson also had to leave a game in September in the third inning in a hoax involving one of his children. A telephone caller said, "Jackie's little girl is going to the hospital. She's real sick," according to Walter Alston. Fortunately, his children were safe but it was a cruel, further distraction to a tough season.

That very game also saw one of the strangest homeruns hit at Ebbets Field. Duke Snider hit a ball that bounced off the right –center field wall (near the exit gate) and into the lower center field stands. Snider, who hit his 37th homerun of the season in the Dodger 10-1 win of the Cardinals, thought the ball hit the tiny ledge in the middle of the wall. Thanks to a previous discussion with another umpire and Dodger shortstop Reese, the possibility of such a play was discussed in the ground rules before the game. "It's still not written down on the ground-rule card. But it's official," Reese said. "We go over it every day," Reese added. "As long as the ball didn't hit the ground it was a homer."

Hurricane Edna caused the Dodgers to start an afternoon game at 5:30 pm on September 11. The ground crew had been given special bonuses (from Walter O'Malley) for spending all night and morning standing on the $14,000 tarpaulin so it wouldn't blow away plus making sure the rest of the field was playable. A crowd of 7,748 saw the Dodgers beat the Milwaukee Braves 5-3 and take over second place 4 ½ games out of first place with 13 games to go in the season. Unfortunately, it was too late for the Dodgers to storm past the Giants. Although the Dodgers finished five games behind the Giants, there was hope for next year.

The Giants had clinched the pennant in late September when rookie pitcher Karl Spooner arrived at Ebbets Field. Spooner struck out the first six Giants he faced and finished with 15 k's and a shutout. In his next start, Spooner shut out the Pittsburgh Pirates and struck out 12 batters.

On November 17 there was a story by Los Angeles Herald –Express writer John Old that there were tentative plans to switch the Dodgers to Los Angeles and that the plans were "hush, hush" and a special meeting was to be held in L.A. on November 22. National League President Warren Giles and Brooklyn Vice-President Fresco Thompson both denied the report. The Brooklyn Junior Chamber of Commerce quickly organized a drive to "keep the Dodgers in Brooklyn". Old stuck to his story and told his readers "to look for and expect vigorous denials" concerning the possible move. "Walter O'Malley, Brooklyn President, has long eyed Los Angeles as a possible future home of the Dodgers," Old said. "…the special meeting quietly arranged without previously publicity was called to offset the urging of Cleveland's Hank Greenberg that the American League expand to 10 cities at the earliest possible opportunity."

Time appeared to be running out for Ebbets Field and the Brooklyn franchise.

Chapter 9   Favorite Dodger Players

Because there was no free agency while the Dodgers played in Brooklyn, players tended to stay on teams at the owner's whim. For good teams, like the Dodgers, this meant they often had a set lineup and a key group of players that they fans got to know personally over many years at Ebbets Field.

Jack Foley's favorite player was Jackie Robinson. "He changed the game. Jackie would throw pitchers off when he was on the bases. He'd dance half way to home plate when he was on third. We didn't have any prejudice in those days, we loved him. We were just kids," Foley said.

Jack's most exciting moment at Ebbets Field came when Gil Hodges was in a tremendous slump. It was a so bad even a priest Father Herbert Redmond of Brooklyn's St. Francis Xavier implored his congregation to pray for him in June of 1953. "Gil was something like 0 for 48 when he came up to bat and the fans gave him a great ovation. You cheered for them instead of booed. It brought tears to my eyes and then he got a hit," Foley said. "Back then, the Dodgers were part of your family. You'd see players on the street and many lived in the neighborhood. Even when Sal Maglie (hated rival) joined the Dodgers, he was welcomed with open arms'" said Foley

Foley now lives in Saline, Michigan and owns a uniform company. He says when the Dodgers moved "it was like your parents were getting divorced". The Captain Pee Wee Reese was a hero to many and honored as such. "On Pee Wee Reese Night, I remember them stopping the game and asking everyone to light the candle that they gave us when we entered the park," Barry Becher said. "They turned the lights out and it was an awesome sight seeing about 35,000 candles burning in the dark night," Becher said. "We all sang happy birthday to Pee Wee with Gladys Goodding belting it out on the organ. I also remember that the car he picked (or his daughter picked) was the cheapest one that was offered to him that night. "I think they offered him about five cars and he picked out a Chevy (not the Cadillac or Chrysler)," said Barry. "His daughter Barbara did pick the car key out of a hat. Everyone wanted him to win the Buick but of course he won the Chevy," fan Paul Warner said. "I'm pretty sure we sang 'Happy Birthday' during the seventh inning stretch," Warner adds.

Pee Wee Reese beats out a bunt in 1956 World Series

Jim Gaffey got quite a surprise the very next day outside of Ebbets Field. "My friends and I actually used the lots around Ebbets as our 'home fields' against neighboring blocks teams like the Sterling St. guys (our chief nemesis)," said Jim Gaffey. "We were using one of these lots and waiting for Sterling Street to show up to answer our challenge when two guys whistled us over to them near two station wagons parked close to the stadium," Gaffey said. "The night before was Pee Wee Reese Night," he said. "It was Pee Wee and Duke Snider wanting help to load many boxed gifts (way before big ticket items-they were toaster, etc.) into the cars. "For doing this, they gave us fifty cents each and a ticket (11 of us) for an upcoming game. For a bunch of us bleacher kids this was a real treat. "We got to sit in the fifth row behind the visitor dugout,' Jim said. "We must have looked a sight with our T-shirts and jeans and Keds with holes in them among all the business suits (the older men always use to wear dress clothes to go to games)." Gaffey said.

"I remember Pee Wee Reese hit a ball into the netting on the right field wall and it got stuck there for a ground rule double," Robert Lerner said. "A couple of innings later, another ball was hit into the netting and both balls came down. "The right fielder did not know which ball was the right ball and there was a big argument," Lerner said. Jackie Robinson also gained a loyal following over the years.

"On Friday, April 11th (1947), I was walking south on Bedford Avenue on my way to Erasmus Hall High School, where I was a freshman, "Robert Gruber said. "As I passed Martense Street, a young black man in a late model car stopped and, in a distinct voice, asked me, "Excuse me fella, which way to Ebbets Field? I replied, 'Keep going about a dozen blocks up Bedford, you can't miss it," Gruber said. "As he thanked me, I realized that it was Jackie Robinson. He was to play as a Dodger for the first time that afternoon (in an exhibition game against the Yankees). As Jackie pulled away, I was too excited to shout encouragement. When I told the story in the school lunch room that day, the few black kids there came over and shook my hand," Gruber said. Fred Harber noticed that the players had to come out of Ebbets Field and cross the street to get to their cars. "We used to wait at the players exit and accost them for their autographs," Harber remembers. "I was reaching into Jackie Robinson's passenger side window and like magic it started to go up! "I had never seen automatic windows before. He saw that I was too startled to remove my hand and he took my scorecard and gave me an autograph, "Fred Harber said.

J. Robinson warming up with teammates

Brian Strum saw "Jackie Robinson leaving Ebbets Field and walking toward his car parked on a gas station lot. It was a convertible. "We surrounded the car after he got in and asked for autographs. He looked perturbed and maybe disturbed," Strum said. "Just then a cop approached telling us to 'beat it' (and in those days when a cop said 'jump', you asked 'how high?') but Jackie said it was okay, just have them make an orderly line and he would sign for each of us (there must have been 20 of us). "And he did. For some reason, I gave him the game program to sign on the back and I still have it," he said. "I remember being thrilled all the way home because in addition to signing for each of us, he shook hands with each of us. It was one of the greatest days I ever had at Ebbets Field," Strum said. Dodger beat writer Dave Anderson remembers a story about "when Jackie Robinson was at UCLA and he was on the baseball team that in the seventh inning if he wasn't going to get up to bat that inning, he'd take off his spikes, go across the street, put on his track shoes, win the long jump (in one jump) and come back and finish the game. I don't know if that's true but that's what was said," Anderson recalled. Hall Of Fame broadcaster Ernie Harwell recalled a scene of Robinson in 1948. "When I was there, it was only the second year. It was still going on…when we'd get on the bus the black people were gathering around the bus. Jackie was sort of a messiah for them. And they were only interested in Jackie, a lot more than they were the team," Harwell remembers. "When I went over to the Giants, we had some good black players like Monte Irvin and Willie Mays but by then they were just major leaguers. You didn't get the same feeling of messiahship that Jackie engendered in everybody," said Harwell.

Gil Hodges was known as the strong, silent type who was originally from Indiana. "I thought Gil was, not only in baseball but in life, one of the true gentlemen. I mean he was outstanding," said teammate Ed Roebuck. "When Gil came up to the Dodgers around '47 or '48, he was a big, shy Indiana farm boy who didn't drink or smoke," Paul Ansbro said. "He was a practicing Catholic also. Everybody drank in those days but Gil went to the bars with the "boys of summer" and drank milk or soda," Ansbro adds. "If you remember Hugh Casey, a relief pitcher with the Dodgers (he once threw one pitch and won a world series game), had a bar on Flatbush Ave. in Brooklyn called Hugh Casey's Chop House. "The place was actually owned by a friendly 'Bookie' named Charley Wagner, who couldn't get a liquor license because of his gambling arrests. The ball players liked the place because it was near Ebbets Field and the drinks and food were usually free. (Ballplayers were notoriously cheap). Gil is there one night sipping a soft drink and in comes Hank Berman (one of the starting pitchers) with a date. Berman introduces his girl, Joan, to Gil and it was love at first sight," Ansbro said. "She was from "Pigtown" and they started dating and eventually married. They moved to Bedford Ave. some years later and Gil became a partner in a bowling alley named after him. "As a patrolman, I went to the alleys every week to bowl and we would chat with Gil who was gracious (especially with our kids)," Ansbro said. "He would sign autographs and sit down and just talk to the kids in a fatherly way," Ansbro added.

"Gil Hodges really took care of me," Bob Aspromonte said, while thinking about his first joining the Dodgers fresh out of high school in 1956. "When you're a 17 year old kid you really didn't belong there. But that's the way they signed you," he said. "I have very special, fond memories of him (Hodges). He made sure I felt fairly comfortable," Aspromonte said.

Don Newcombe was the first black All Star starting pitcher and ace of the Dodger staff. "Once, we took the then - ferry from 69th Street in Bay Ridge to Staten Island after a game," Charles Heffernan said. "Dodger pitcher Don Newcombe was on the boat (he lived in New Jersey and crossed Staten Island on the way home). Although he'd lost the game that day, he was gracious in giving me an autograph," Heffernan said.

"I spent lots of Saturdays, holidays, nights, etc. at Ebbets Field," said Donald Morin. About half of them were with my father. We loved to watch Newcombe and Campanella work together," Morin said. "Campy was a great target for Newk. We never could see his fast ball… just a cloud of smoke. What a pair they were," said Morin. Roy Campanella became the National League's MVP three times during his career with the Dodgers and the great handler of its pitching staff. Art Weiss got to know Dodger catcher Roy Campanella well. "Mr. Roy Campanella was a gentleman's gentleman" Weiss said. "I got to sit in his lap during warm up games. He knew that I had polio and had difficulty walking. He knew my Uncle Ray and visited me in the hospital. I loved that man and visited him often after his accident. A true role model for me," Art adds.

Joe Medwick

Fred Harber was waiting outside the player's exit at Ebbets Field when "Roy Campanella came out and a kid grabbed his hand. "His ring came off and rolled down the street. I was closest to it and went after it." Fred said. "I saw Roy almost make a dash toward me, but he realized I was not going to run away with it. It was 2-3 times too big for my thumb! "When he shook hands with me, he completely engulfed my hand in his," Harber said.

George Shuba was a good looking outfielder with the Dodgers that caught many kid's eyes with his acrobatic catches. "I remember George Shuba catching fly balls behind his back," Barry Becher said. "I thought that was great. I went home and practiced for hours throwing my Spaldeen up in the air and trying to catch it behind my back. It took a long time but I learned how to do it," Becher said. "On the day of the All Star game, the balance of the team used to practice in the morning. Jake Pitler, the first base coach, used to take a couple of us in and allow us to shag fly balls in the outfield. It was great to be out there," Stan Roth said.

"I also remember watching George Shuba fielding fly balls in the outfield during batting practice. He was a wiz at fielding them behind his back," said Roth. "At one game, I bought tickets for 50 cents each with a friend who had a broken arm. We were talking with George Shuba, a Dodger outfielder, when my friend threw Shuba an orange and in return he threw a baseball up to him," Robert Lerner said.

George "Shotgun" Shuba (now 79) no longer answers mail from fans but that's partially due to "his loss of hearing and not wanting to pick and chose among the many letters and requests he constantly gets" according to his son Mike. Shuba basks in the glory of being the first man to shake Jackie Robinson's hand at home plate in Montreal on April 18, 1946. That's the day, Jackie hit his first professional homerun and George Shuba was the white man (next to bat) that welcomed him home. Mike Shuba believes that was the point when the color barrier in baseball really was broken. George Shuba had a positive addiction to hitting that was honed by his swinging a weighted bat 500 times at a string hung from a ceiling indoors on rainy days. His nickname referred at first to his arm but later his bat did the blasting after an explosive snap of his wrists as they propelled the bat through the ball.

Fred Nash remembers Gene Hermanski "hitting three home runs in one game and also him making a diving catch in left field and starting a triple play. He was a good hitter, a fair fielder and terrible on ground balls that were hit to him in left field. I also remember him having a weight builder's physique," Fred said.

"Joe Havens was a detective in the 70th Pct. and one of the first baseball coaches I ever had. On the first day, he told me 'If you want to learn to play this game right, watch Jim Gilliam'," Bernie McCoy said. "You always listen to Coach (particularly your first one) so every time I went to Ebbets Field I watched Gilliam not just the way he hit and fielded but the way he backed up plays he wasn't involved in," McCoy said. "I always wondered 'Is this guy being appreciated?" Bernie said.

Billy Cox came over from the Pirates and was a solid defensive third baseman. "I remember how excited I was to go to the game and the players seemed so talented back then," Jack Skelly said. "I don't think I ever saw a ball get by Billy Cox on third and Dixie Walker used to wear out the grass in one spot in right field just by walking back and forth in one spot (maybe a strip 6 feet long and 2 feet wide)," Skelly said.

"The Dodgers had a third baseman named Billy Cox. "He was so slight in build that he looked like a wind would knock him over but he was a great fielder with a strong arm,' Robert Lerner said. "When a ball was hit to him, he would catch it, twirl it in his hands and then throw the runner out by a step,"

Lerner said Carl Furillo became a magician with how he was able to play balls hit off the concave wall in right field. While other fielders looked puzzled, Furillo had an uncanny knack of knowing where each ball would go and with his deadly throwing arm, gunned down many runners who challenged his ability. "When Furillo went to right, I loved to see him pretend he was going to catch a fly ball (when all the time he knew it was off the wall), then quickly turn around and play the ball perfectly and some times throw the guy out at first," Jack Skelly said.

Paul Warner had an unusual experience while visiting Ebbets Field with his two buddies Donnie Riconda and Ronnie Polo in 1954. They went to see the Dodgers play a double header against the Cubs. "After we win the first game easily there's about an hour before the second game starts," Warner says. "With a lot of people milling around, we head for left field and vault over the black, wrought iron picket fence to the grandstands. When we get to the left field line, we head down the ramp to get closer to the field. At ground level, we come upon a fence that's been pushed around and gives a bit." Warner said. "We squeeze our way under and head for third base seats. We notice a bunch of empty seats behind the Dodger dugout…WOW. We keep going all the way around toward first base. We find three empty seats right behind the dugout-we're in heaven! The players come out and we're starting to feel like we belong there. We don't know if anyone is coming back to these seats or maybe they've gone for the day. All of a sudden, out of nowhere, right before the Bums take the field, I feel a hand on my shoulder and I know we're in trouble," Warner explains. "It's an attendant and he wants to see our tickets. We're all set to move when a head pops out of the dugout. It's Carl Furillo and he calls over to the guard and gestures to him. He says a few words in the guy's ear, the guy smiles and walks away," Warner says. "Skoonj" (Furillo's nickname because he loved to eat squid) had saved the day. We watched the whole game in those box seats," Warner added. Warner worked 24 years on Wall Street first as an otc stock trader and then as a gold trader. He now works for the Treasury Department at West Point, lives in New Hampton, New York and hopes to retire soon.

"After I slept out overnight at Ebbets Field, I got my seat in the boxes in the bleachers. (General admission was about 75 cents for that World Series game). "I threw a bag of peanuts down to Duke Snider," said Morton LaPayover. "He emptied the peanuts into his pocket, but a ball in the bag and threw it back up to me," LaPayover said. LaPayover also got to meet a Dodger legend completely by accident. "When I was about ten years old, my sister worked for Austin Nichols (liquor distributor in

Brooklyn). One of the salesmen was a man named Leon Cadore. I was totally shocked when I learned that he had pitched a complete 26 inning game against the Boston Braves a number of years earlier. I thought he was lying to me," LaPayover said.

"I just talked to Cadore that one day for about five or ten minutes. He was very nice but didn't appreciate my doubting that he had pitched 26 innings. I did not believe it until I looked it up in my 'bible'- the book of baseball stats that I loved to read," LaPayover said. Nat Mushkin lived on Washington Avenue in Crown Heights. Across Washington Ave., his six-story apartment building faced the Brooklyn Botanical Gardens. In the other direction, two blocks behind his building was Ebbets Field. "Every Saturday and Sunday morning, when the Dodgers were playing at home, all of us boys would walk to the big, marble rotunda and wait for Leo Durocher and the coaches to come to the ballpark," Mushkin said. "This was an important part of autograph collecting since the coaches would occasionally take baseballs from us (with our names), get them signed by the players in the locker room, and return them to us after the game," Mushkin said. "An indelible memory of Durocher during the late 1930's was of him sweeping into the rotunda with his entourage dressed like a Hollywood personality," Mushkin said.

Jeanne Dolan enjoyed watching Leo Durocher at Ebbets Field. "We always tried to get seats between home and first base because we could then see the Dodger's dugout and could enjoy seeing firsthand some of Durocher's antics during the game," she said. "And hardly a game went by that he didn't challenge a call from the home plate umpire, complete with nose-to-nose 'in your face' confrontations. Durocher would kick dirt over home plate making it necessary for the umpire to bend down with his whisk broom and clean the plate…only to have Lippy kick the dirt again and again." said Dolan.

"I was born and raised in Brooklyn and during the ages of six to 12 lived on Fennimore Street a stone's throw from Ebbets Field,' Kathleen Cassidy Hardy said. "My brothers would grab their gloves and we would walk up to Ebbets Field and stand out on Bedford Avenue, I guess waiting for balls over the wall. "We got to know where Pee Wee Reese, Duke Snider and Gil Hodges parked their cars (behind the garage on Bedford Ave), " Cassidy Hardy said. "We would wait for the players to come out. I remember Don Newcombe would always have a cab waiting for him," Hardy said.

"Well, one day the kids were pushing and I got knocked over and hurt my ankle. What I didn't know at the time, a guy named Jake Pitler (coach) picked me up and asked if I was alright. ," Cassidy Hardy said. "After that, every time he came out he would come over and say hello and sometimes we would walk him down to Flatbush Ave. where he took the train," Cassidy Hardy added. "Well my oldest brother Peter wanted to take advantage of my new found friend and told me to ask him for an autographed baseball. Sure enough, the next time he came out he handed me a ball. The autograph on the ball was 'Sandy Koufax'," Cassidy Hardy said. "My brother was very upset and said, 'who is he', " Cassidy Hardy said. "Well it wasn't too long after that, that we found out who he was become in LA. "That's my Ebbets Field story and a very favorite Brooklyn memory for me."

Bil Phifer waited until autograph seekers would die down as players would walk to their cars after a game was over. "I would walk behind the horde until it dwindling down. Eventually, we were alone to talk and get to know each other on a one on one basis all the way to his car," Phifer said. "On many occasions, we would get a bonus… a ride home in the player's car. The personal relationships that I developed were with Billy Cox, Joe Hatten, Tommy Brown, Carl Erskine, Preacher Roe, Erv Palica, Gil Hodges and for a short time Chuck Connors," Phifer said. "When I would meet one of them at his car and walk with him to the ballpark, other kids would see us chatting and wonder who I was …and how far had I come with him… and did I live in his neighborhood …or what? "Of course, I would never tell. I would just say that he was my friend, " Phifer said.

Frances Costello Flaherty got a thrill from a Dodger while at work. "I was 16 years old and working after school at the Methodist Hospital and PeeWee Reese's wife had a baby there and I got his autograph. My father was so excited, he had to take the piece of paper with him to show all his friends," Costello Flaherty said.

Pete Reiser arrived in the big leagues with Pee Wee Reese in 1940. They were nicknamed "The Gold Dust twins" and great things were expected of them. While Harry Rudolph was a Dodger batboy from 1945–47, he became friendly with Pete Reiser. "Pete Reiser…he kind of liked me. He would always play what they call 'burnout' with me. So we were playing catch and he could throw with either hand. God he could throw as far left handed as he could right handed. He always got a hold of me and he says 'come on we'll play burnout'. So he'd throw it as hard at me and it was usually behind the batting cage where the pitchers used to warm up in those days," said Rudolph. One day, I figure "I'm really going to throw this sucker back to him' and it sailed over his head and hit Auggie Galen in the head and knocked him out. You know I'm like jeese…I'm finished but Auggie Galen didn't get mad at me and I kept my job," Rudolph laughed.

Another unfortunate event occurred later that year to Reiser. "Pete was sliding back to first base on a pick off throw and I heard his leg snap when it broke," said Rudolph. New York Times writer Dave Anderson's favorite Dodger when he was a kid was Pete Reiser. "Pete Reiser, of course you know, kept running into walls and getting hurt. It was a tragedy. He was never the same player. He would have been in the Hall of Fame," Anderson said. "He won the batting title when he was a rookie. He was fast and often stole home … he was just developing. He would have been a power hitter and hit a lot of homeruns," adds Anderson. "I don't say he would have hit 40 or 50 but he would have hit 30 which in those days was a good year," said Anderson. Dodger fan Don Schorr remembers "sitting along the Dodger bullpen one day". "Billy Cox was the bullpen catcher that day and he was warming up a very, very nervous rookie who had yet to play his first game. There was a signal from the mound and Cox said to the shaky rookie, 'They want you kid'." The pitcher walked unsteadily to the mound and into history… His name? Carl Erskine," said Schorr. Erskine went on to pitch 12 years for the Dodgers and post a 122-78 record with two no hitters. Don Schorr remembers Tommy Brown and "his potential was such that Brooklyn organization signed him as a 'bonus baby' for $10,000 (an enormous figure in those days) right out of high school, bypassing farm club experience." He was the best batting practice hitter on the team. I remember one after another hit into the stands. But in games, he just could not produce and after a few season, he was out of baseball," said Schorr.

Norm Kuirland, who writes the Flatbush Faithful newsletter, met one of his heroes in an odd fashion. "On my route home from school one day, I walked by Ebbets Field and on Bedford Avenue there was a large gate, and I was looking through it. This guy came up behind me and asked what I was doing. I told him I was kinda looking at the field. I said I just wanted to see if there were any ballplayers I knew. He said he was a ball player and I said I didn't know him. He said 'Well, my name is Sandy Koufax'. He explained who he was (a rookie pitcher) and I got his autograph," Kuirland said.

Chapter 10   Workers at Ebbets Field

Happy Felton's Knothole Gang was seen on WOR Ch.9 from April 21, 1950 until August 24, 1957. Happy was a former vaudeville, stage and radio comic actor and band leader who hosted the show for grade school ball players. Looking like a large set smiling Sgt. Bilko in a Dodger uniform, Happy typically would have three boys from local teams compete in a fielding contest judged by a Brooklyn Dodger. In the only remaining kinescope tape still in existence (by A Rare Sportsfilms) captures Tuesday evening June 26, 1956, Happy introduces each boy from St. Bernadette's baseball program which has 400 plus boys participating in it. The action takes place in and along the stands past first base and by the Dodger bullpen. After each boy and his manager is introduced, a trustee Fred Gresch of the Lincoln Savings Bank is interviewed and makes a pitch for his band instrument program for the schools by declaring "the boy who blows a horn won't blow a safe". Happy and his sidekick (Bucky) hand out a Dodger cap, yearbook and autographed bat to each boy.

Jackie Robinson appears and answers a question from each boy then starts playing catch after they warm up with two tosses from Happy who tells one boy "don't throw the ball through me". After a few minutes of playing catch in right field with Jackie, the boys come back in the stands and each receives a savings account from the trustee, Mr. Gresch. Jackie Robinson returns to announce the night's winner and consoles each loser.

Happy Felton then corrals the previous night's winner Ronald Ferrari and takes a long walk down the foul line with mike in hand talking all the way. All this is done live and apparently without cue cards. Once Happy arrives at home plate and gets situated in front of another camera, Pee Wee Reese bounds out of the dugout to answer questions. Pee Wee gives advice on bunting, hitting behind a runner and making the toughest play for a third baseman. Happy congratulates the boy once again and lets Pee Wee take him into the Dodger dugout to meet all his heroes. The show ends with Happy asking folks to support the other sponsors - Charles Keisler Oldsmobile dealer and Davega food stores and mentions he has an after- the-game show.

The Knothole Gang show was good public relations for the Dodgers and it was hoped would help boost young ballplayers as well. Mike Doherty was on the Happy Felton Show in April 1956. "Junior Gilliam was the Dodger who ran us through some trails and I was lucky enough to be picked as best player and got to come back the next day and speak to whomever I wanted on the Dodgers. I picked Duke Snider. I got to sit in the dugout and met most of the Dodgers who signed the baseball I

Batboys C.C. Giovanni & Bil Phifer surround Happy Felton

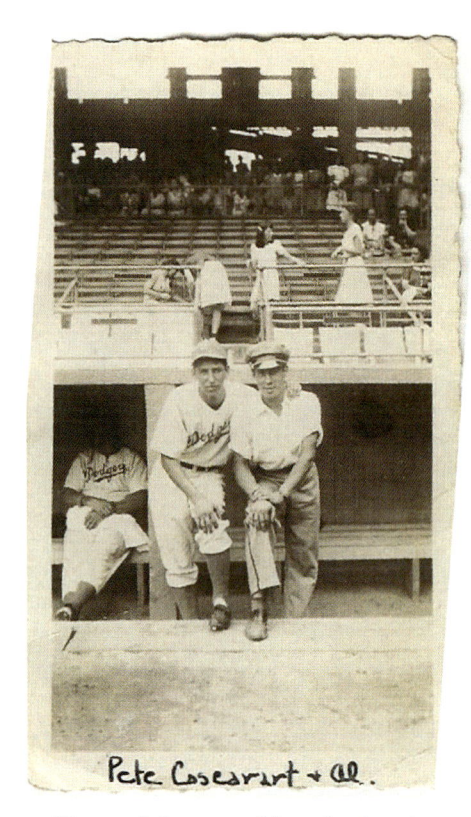

Groundskeeper Alex Arahovites with infielder Pete Coscarart.

was presented with the previous day. That ball is sitting on top of my TV in a glass case," Doherty said. "The last show of every year he (Happy) had the two batboys on TV," says ex batboy Bil Phifer. "We would throw them (kids from local teams) some balls, play catch, throw ground balls and pick a winner. Then they would ask us questions', said Phifer.

"Happy Felton also had a post game show where the stars of the game (I think one from each team) appeared, spoke about the game and answered questions which were either called in or sent via mail," Alan Greenberg remembers. "My father once won a box of Tydol Oil Company products and tickets to a game for having a question selected and then answered by Roy Campanella. "I understand, but can't confirm, that Felton was not the jolly fellow in real life that he appeared to be on TV," according to Alan Greenberg

George Colligan tells a story of the orange drink vendor who actually looked like Happy Felton. "He roamed the left field bleachers selling orange drink. And everyone called him "Happy Felton"…"Hey Happy Felton…" you know the drill. One day… in the broiling sun, he suddenly snapped. He had enough "Hey Happy Felton…" and tossed his back pack of orange soda all over a couple of guys who were really on his case," Colligan said.

Mary Nolan Bregman's dad (Joe Nolan) was an usher at Ebbets Field. "I was nine years old when the Dodgers left Brooklyn. My father, however, would bring me to games for a couple of years prior to their leaving. My dad would naturally be in the park a couple of hours prior to the game. I was able to watch practices for both teams. After the start of the game, he would move me around as the ticket holders came for their seats and all the other ushers would keep an eye on me just to make sure all was ok. Before the start of the games, he would bring me into the dugouts of both the visiting team and our beloved Dodgers and introduced me to some of the players," Bregman said. "I remember thinking how "old" they were, but all, without exception, were extremely nice and patient with a shy, little girl whose father was extremely proud of her. My dad also sat me next to Happy Felton's gang during the broadcast. All the boys were upset when I caught a ball during the actual game- well, really, it landed next to me and I picked it up. My dad had the players autograph it for me. I wasn't that I was all that interested in the games-just happy to spend the day with my dad at his second job and enjoyed the small park adventure," Mary said.

"I remember a batboy named Al Levy. He went under the name of Al Levey as he felt being Jewish would not be beneficial to his job," fan Bob Gottdenker said. "The Dodger batboy pay was very nominal perhaps $5 per game but he would get some tips. He would also try to get some balls, forge the player's autographs (which he became proficient at) and sell them. This must have been 1943-44 when I would sometimes help Al Levy after a game. We would take the bats out of the rack adjacent to the dugout, carry them through the dugout and tunnel to outside the clubhouse where we would put them in a huge truck or container. That was a thrill for a 13 year old "Al became friendly with Roscoe McGowen, a sportswriter of renown with the NY Times. McGowen got Levy a position with the Times Sports department and he left his batboy job," according to Bob Gottdenker.

Art Weiss's Uncle Raymond Haber was "the Pretzel Man" who stood outside of Ebbets Field selling his five cent pretzels. "Uncle Ray was a man who went to all ballgames around the city and knew each player. He got to know all the players and anytime there were home games, he would get me passes to get inside. "I sat in Carl Furillo's lap, was hugged many times by Campy and Duke always waved to me in the stands just above the dugout and Dimaggio of the Yankees gave me an old glove," Weiss said. "My Uncle Ray was a small man with a big heart".

Sophia Tsoupas's grandfather Alexander Arahovites was a groundskeeper at Ebbets Field in the 40's. "He was friends with a with a lot of the players and he owned the parking lots and hot dog stands outside of Ebbets Field," Tsoupas said. "He used to make the pitcher's mound," she said. Sophia has several photos of Dodgers with her grandfather at Ebbets Field. "One I have with me right now is my grandfather with Pete Coscarart in 1940. It's at Ebbets Field because my grandpa is in his groundskeeper uniform. Then we have another picture of Vito Tamulis standing in the dugout. Pee Wee Reese is in the dugout and some players in back of him," Sophia said. "Then we have Harry Lavagetto in the dugout also," she said.

"My father was a cabdriver and he picked up Stan Musial and Marty Marion in his cab," Robert Lerner said. "He asked Stan what he thought he would do if he played for the Dodgers and he replied, '.375 average, 50 home runs and 150 RBI's'," Lerner said. It was someone like Lerner's cab driving father who inspired sport's cartoonist Willard Mullin's famous Brooklyn Dodger Bum. In 1937, while taking a cab back from a Dodgers game, Mullin heard the cab driver ask, "How'd our bums do today?" Mullin went back to his New York World Telegram paper and created his award winning character. Jimmy Mueller, and his buddies were inspired in another way by a Dodger. "We had a guy in our neighborhood

Groundkeeper at work

named "Duke" who was a groundskeeper at Ebbets Field. He would get us down to get autographs from the players before the games," said Mueller. "I remember that during one season, Duke Snider had made an offhand remark to the press about the Dodgers not deserving to win the pennant," Mueller said. "For the rest of the season, any game we went to, we made sure we got close as possible to center field so we could tell the Duke what we thought of his remark,' Mueller said.

"To supplement his salary, my father had a part-time job on weekends and night games as a ticket taker and, after a few years, as a ticket seller at Ebbets Field," Bil Phifer said. "Since he got his job during the 'Great Depression', he was always grateful to have it…particularly with four kids at home to feed and clothe. As a result, he didn't want my brother Artie and me hanging around Ebbets Field getting into trouble or worse getting him into trouble," Phifer said. "We honored his wishes until the time Artie was thirteen and I was eleven. That was the summer of 1947 when the magnetism of Ebbets Field became too great for two young Brooklyn boys," Phifer said.

Harold Seymour noticed that in the twenties, "We could even work to get in, picking up papers in the stands before the park opened to earn bleacher passes. "These were handwritten on strips of pink paper and handed out by one of the owners, Steve McKeever as he sat on a camp chair holding his gold-handled blackthorn. We could also turn a stile for fifty cents and get a seat in the grandstand around the fifth inning depending on the size of the crowd. We might even work up on the old fashioned scoreboard in left field by pulling ropes weighted with bricks to post numbers while watching the game through one of the slots," Seymour said

Before Joe McDonald became a General Manager for the New York Mets, he was a ticket taker at gate 19. "It was a famous gate because well … the owners, reporters, players, the managers many of them would walk through that gate and I was privileged to service them as a young 19-20 year old lad," McDonald said. Gate 19 was "First gate on the left as you went into the famous rotunda. It (rotunda) was a big part of my life… It would be a glorious experience I would think as you walked into that privileged are. That was more for the reserved seat section. It wasn't for the general admission," McDonald added. During the fifteen years he worked there (1942 until 1957), McDonald saw many kids sneak in. "Yea they would climb up the wall in left field…challenge it that way. I've seen many kids fortunately I never saw one fall…they were quite acrobatic. They were amazing. They would hide in the men's bathroom until the gates opened. You had to hide …because otherwise they would toss you out," McDonald said.

One of the guys who would do the tossing would be the dreaded security guard Joe Moore. "I looked at his big, ugly puss for so many years. He was gigantic. His waistline had to be like 50. He was huge and was not the kindliness of characters but I guess he performed his job admirably," McDonald said.

According to McDonald, Ebbets Field didn't undergo a lot of changes. "I think it kept its unique beauty. Certainly, nobody tinkered with the right field wall. The one thing they did do was bring in the left field seats to make it more inviting for Pafko, Hodges and Campanella," McDonald said. "Not that it cheapened that much but adding those box seats in left field was the most radical change that I could see. The upper stands, lower stands and press box I suspect stayed the same," McDonald noted.

Although many folks dislike O'Malley, McDonald has nothing but nice things to say about him. "Walter was always fine with me, his wife was a doll. She had a speech…not an impediment but a voice problem. God, she was a charming woman…when she talked …you could hardly hear her…she was a doll," McDonald said. McDonald started out on the bottom rung. "Actually, when I started for three years I made fifty cents a day as a stile boy. It was all worth it. I was preparing myself (I didn't know it at the time) for a career in baseball. I had the privilege of observing some tremendous players…who played the game right. I was very fortunate because I was already studying how the game should be played," McDonald said.

Hall of Fame broadcaster Ernie Harwell got his major league career started during the 1948 season after Red Barber was felled with a perforated ulcer. He was announcing the minor league Atlanta Cracker's games when he was traded for Dodger Catcher Cliff Dapper.

"The people of Brooklyn were very receptive to me. I could not have asked for better treatment. They were very hospitable, warm and friendly. It was a wonderful experience. I'd just come in cold in the middle of the season. I didn't know anybody and everyone was just open and completely warm about everything," Harwell said. Harwell enjoyed the facilities at Ebbets Field. "Oh they (facilities) were great. We were very close, real close much like Tiger Stadium was. We were right back of the plate and had a great view. Of course, Ebbets Field was sort of a band box of a park anyways. Everyone was down close to the players. That was part of its charm," Harwell said. One quirk at Ebbets Field Harwell took part in was with a sponsor. "A guy would hit a homerun and we'd send a carton of Old Gold (cigarettes) down the screen. Tex Rickard was the old p.a. announcer and he'd come out and get it and hand it out to the player that hit the homerun," Harwell said. Rickard himself was a character according to Ernie. "Tex was 55-60 years old. He was a fairly short and stocky guy. No matter what the temperature was, he wore that Dodger sweater. It was a white sweater with the name DODGERS written across it. "He was pretty good with the malapropos," Harwell noted. Rickard's most famous screw up was, "Will the ladies and gentlemen in the centerfield bleachers please remove their clothing" after an umpire wanted him to have the fans remove their coats and jackets from railings they were draped over.

Another goof up was, "Attention, ladies and gentlemen, a little boy has been found lost." Harwell recalled another time after Jimmy Powers, a reporter for the Daily News, complained that the Dodgers didn't announce things on the p.a. that people heard on the radio. "You know a guy on the radio gets much more information about changes and things like that, said Harwell.

"So Preacher Roe was pitching against the Cardinals and they got something like four or six runs in the first inning and knocked him out. Tex gets on and says, 'Preacher Roe has left the game because he doesn't feel good,'" Harwell laughs.

Even though Harwell was a southerner, he had no misgivings about Jackie Robinson being on the Dodgers. "I was with a lot of black people in the service and I think that sort of broke down any barriers that I may have had. You know I was a Christian and I accepted it. It wasn't any big deal for me," Harwell said. "Jack had a great personality and you had to admire the way he handled things on the advice of Rickey, you turn the other cheek and take all the physical and mental abuse that was directed to him," said Harwell. Harwell believes that Robinson's arrival in the major leagues "was the most significant thing that's happened in sports history. "It opened the door for not only baseball but all the Latin players and all the guys in all the sports," Harwell continued.

Harwell went on to broadcast for the New York Giants, Baltimore Orioles and Detroit Tigers after his initial break with the Dodgers. He now lives in Michigan with his wife Lulu and he still does commercials and attends many charity functions in his "retirement".

Harry Rudolph was working at Yankee Stadium at the press gate when he met Dodger's clubhouse man John "Senator" Griffin during an exhibition game between the two teams in 1945. "So I just asked him if they had a batboy. He said 'Yea, I think we do but why don't you come over to Ebbets Field just in case the kid doesn't show up'. I got over there early and got to see Johnny Griffin and the kid never showed up," Rudolph said. "I got paid a dollar a game. I worked a minimum of ten to twelve hours a day. You had to be there early. I had to saddle soap every shoe and hang up stuff in the dryer, the jockstraps and sweatshirts. I had to put clean towels in the lockers, and then come back in the morning and take all the stuff out of the dryer and make sure it was in the locker before the guy showed up," said Rudolph. "I had to sweep out the locker room and then I had to mop the shower you know before you go home," he said. "I autographed every freaking baseball too. My specialty was Pee Wee Reese, Pete Reiser and Leo Durocher. I can still do them perfectly right now. There were about six-dozen balls, you know I had to sign them, the players were sick and tired of signing the damn things. That was part of your job," Rudolph recalls.

Rudolph worked as a batboy when Jackie Robinson broke in. "I was there for the first two months. Jackie dressed next to me. Yea, that was a thrill I mean probably my most exciting time. I didn't realize what the hell was going on," Rudolph said. Rudolph now has a restaurant in La Jolla, California and ex Dodger GM Buzzie Bavasi often stops by.

Bavasi first worked for the Dodgers when he got a job from Larry MacPhail in 1938 and made $35 a week as a "glorified office boy". After earning a Bronze Star in World War II, Bavasi worked his way through the Dodger farm organization and was named Vice-President in 1950 when Walter O'Malley took over as President. He was also given the General Manager's duties as well.

Bavasi remembers how "fun it was playing and going to Ebbets Field. It was a new adventure every day. One of the adventures occurred when "we were threatened by the Musician's Union with a possible picket line if we didn't do two things. We were to pay the Dodger 'Symphoney' a union scale wage and we were to make five box seats available to them, free of charge," Bavasi said. "Keep in mind that the five men making up the little band did it on their own time and because they enjoyed playing during the game. They wanted none of the union threats," he said. "To call the union's bluff, we decided to have a musical night at the ball park. Anyone coming to the park with a musical instrument was admitted free of charge. They came with every type of instrument. The kick off was when seven men came through the gate with an old baby grand piano. The union got the point and left us alone," Bavasi noted.

Thousands showed up with everything from violins, kazoos, drums, trombones horns and of course the piano. Happy Felton was named the director and tried to get everyone to play three songs …"Hail, Hail The Gangs All Here," "Take Me Out To The Ball Game," and "Roll Out The Barrel" before the game started. The visiting Boston Braves were taking batting practice while the noise poured out from the stands and after a final "song" was played, Felton shot off a gun and a dummy was thrown from the upper deck and the Braves almost jumped out of their uniforms.

The umpires pleaded with the Dodgers to make the fans quit playing or they would forfeit the game and the Dodgers replied, "You make 'em quit." The game was played and the Dodgers won. The Musical Appreciation quickly became known as Musical Depreciation night ever after.

Dave Anderson started covering the Dodgers as a beat writer for the Brooklyn Eagle in 1953. He liked the facilities at Ebbets Field. "It was above home plate hanging from the roof there. The radio booth was down below. It was fine for the day to day coverage of that era. When I say that era, I mean the early 50's," said Anderson. "When you had the World Series there naturally you had an auxiliary press box. Press boxes were just not that big in those years in baseball." he said. Anderson had many interviews with Jackie Robinson. "You know Robinson was always involved with some kind of rhubarb as Red Barber used to say. I talked to Robinson a lot. He would always love to talk to you." Anderson remembers. During his years covering the Dodgers, Anderson came to appreciate Jackie Robinson's talent. "I still say he was the best baseball player I ever saw. You can talk about Mantle and all these guys, I never saw Babe Ruth, but I mean as good as Henry Aaron was, and Henry Aaron is to me the next best player to Babe Ruth, if I were picking a team… choosing up sides, I would want Robinson as my first pick," said Anderson. "You know he could beat you so many different ways. He could play so many different positions. He was such a great base runner plus he could disrupt the other team so much. It's a shame he wasn't in the big leagues at age 21 instead of age 28," Anderson noted. "I mean this guy was one of the great athletes in American history. He was all Pacific Coast conference I think in basketball and he was a great half back in football (at UCLA)," Anderson said.

Paul Ansbro's father was a attending physician at a local hospital when a fan (John Christian) arrived one night with broken jaw after Leo Durocher and security guard Joe Moore allegedly administered some frontier justice after the June 8, 1945 night game for the fan's constant heckling

.The Dodgers settled a civil suit for $6,500 and a criminal trial followed. After Ansbro's father had a memory lapse at that trial (over the beating), Paul often was among Dodger celebrities and saw many games courtesy of his father's new benefactors.

One celebrity was Hilda Chester. "Hilda was a character. She was at my parent's home on several occasions with Chuck Dressen and she liked her booze. I know, I was the 'boy bartender'," he said. "She worked for Harry M. Stevens Inc. who had the food franchise at Ebbets Field. She cooked up and served up to game time, then took her seat with her followers in the bleachers," said Ansbro. Chester also testified at Leo Durocher's criminal trial and swore Leo was only protecting her honor from an abusive fan who had called her a "c**k sucker". Tom Knight is Brooklyn's baseball historian and he remembers Hilda Chester. He mentioned that she arrived on the scene about 1939. "Yea, she worked for Stevens. She used to package peanuts. Then she started ringing the cow bell and she became a celebrity but she was really a mental case," said Knight.

Roy Vellia P.A. announcer 1940

Chester would often arrive with a "Hilda is here" sign and cheer her Dodgers on. More than once, she would snake dance through the stands in celebration with other fans. She once was offered a reserve seat by Leo Durocher but she turned it down to sit in the bleachers because "there are the real fans. You can bang the bell all you darn please. The 55 centers don't fuss so much about a little noise," she said.

Chester started ringing the ten cent bell at Ebbets Field in 1937 as part of a prescribed exercise for a stiff arm. Years later, players pitched in and bought her a silver bracelet with a miniature baseball and her name engraved on it. She was elected President of the FlockBusters Club in 1944 A place most fans never heard of at Ebbets Field was called the Greasy Spoon by broadcaster Red Barber. "This is my name for the workroom and kitchen of the four Stevens brothers, the caterers whose father founded the business and invented the hot dog. Hal is the brother who presides at Ebbets Field, and in this kitchen are two rough tables. The Greasy Spoon nestles away from the fans, suspended under the right field

Dorothy and James Kennedy

stands, and next to the umpire's dressing room," Barber noted in his essay My Ten Years With the Dodgers. "Before the games in this one quiet spot at Brooklyn gather the umpires and the writers. This is truly the most exclusive club I have heard about. It is the Steven's kitchen and no money is ever accepted. You belong to baseball when you pull up one of those eight chairs in the Greasy Spoon," said Barber. Barber went on to say he learned a lot of the baseball rules from the umpires he talked with in this room. He also mentioned that Hal Stevens served everyone there himself.

Terry Vellia "grew up next door to Ebbets Field on Montgomery Street". "Way back, my dad (Roy Vellia) was the park announcer. My great uncle was the groundskeeper and my godfather was a batboy," Vellia said. "As a young kid, I can remember my grandparents parking cars for the games in their yard. Homeruns would land in our backyard. Our cat (Pepper) was forever holding up games while they chased him off the field," said Vellia. "We have very few items left but I do have Judge McKeever's cane. He gave it to my grandfather," she said.

"My dad worked for the Brooklyn Eagle and he had a Press Pass that allowed him to go to Ebbets Field for every game," said Dorothy Zaremba. "He used to take me to at least 20 games a season and I actually was able to get on the field with him and meet the players. I was the boy, he never had," she said. "In the early 50's, when I was a kid, we used to put a 3" x 5" index card in the player's suit jackets and they would sign them and mail them back to us," Zaremba recalled. "My dad was assigned to cover the 1955 World Series and I did get to go to a game with him. I still have a team ball signed by the 1955 Dodgers. It is faded now, but still legible and it is a remembrance of a part of my youth that I will never forget," Zaremba said. Zaremba lives with her watercolorist husband Anthony and he has a website with sports art. He has done entire shows on the Brooklyn Dodgers.

Chapter 11   Players Remember Ebbets Field

"When I saw Ebbets Field for the first time as a Brooklyn Dodger. It was love at first sight," said Duke Snider in his book Duke of Flatbush. "I loved that old ballpark and everything about it. And that covered a lot. There was Hilda Chester with her cowbell in the outfield stands. There was a fan named Eddie Battan who used to blow a tin whistle. The Sym-phony band strolled the stands playing Dixieland music, and from his seat Jack Pierce sent up balloons with Cookie Lavagetto's name on them, because Cookie was his favorite player".

"I hit a homerun onto Bedford Avenue on the Sunday afternoon of our last weekend in Ebbets Field" said Snider. "It would be the last home run anyone ever hit there. After the game, I told Walt Alston I didn't want to play the next two-game series against Pittsburgh…I'd hit a home run and I wanted to remember that as my last Ebbets Field experience. I was being torn away from my baseball home, and I wanted to remember her that way. Walt understood".

Outfielder Any Pafko

"Ebbets Field was not a pitcher's park…no foul territory, short right field and short left center field. However, our team usually scored runs there, we seldom got shut out," said Carl Erskine. "Fans were close and could be heard speaking to you from the mound or batter's box. Also the dugouts were easily within shouting distance," Erskine said.

"It was a very intimate park. One of the tough things for a pitcher in Ebbets Field was there was very little foul territory. Most people wouldn't think of that as being any disadvantage but believe me. It kept a lot of hitters alive because the ball (foul) was just barely in the stands and not playable," Erskine said."I'd always heard horror stories about Ebbets Field from a pitching standpoint and a lot of pitchers came in from visiting teams would shy away from pitching there if they could but I had some of my best days at Ebbets Field. Mostly, because I never thought about that being a problem plus the fact that our team too advantage of the short fences pretty well too," said Erskine.

"The other thing of course was the close proximity to the fans. You could hear easy from the mound. You could hear guys calling you and talking to you. I have memories of fans calling me 'Oyskin' and yelling words of encouragement like 'trow it thru his head' and a few things like that.

"You know there were a lot of traditions behind playing there with teams of the past and some of the names that I heard, Dazzy Vance and Van Lingo Mungo and all those names and they'd come back occasionally and sit on the bench and talk to young players about how it used to be," Erskine recalled.

Ebbets Field "always produced a lot of arguments about balls that wedged on the fence or lay on the ledge. "That happened more than once. I was pitching against the Giants one night and Hank Thompson, a little black left handed hitting third baseman, hit a line drive off me and hit the face of the scoreboard and it stuck. Schaeffer Beer had a sign on the face and the H and one of the E's were outlined in neon and they used that for hit and error. Anyways, there was a ground rule that said any ball that stayed on the scoreboard was a homerun. Well, that referred to the top of the scoreboard because there was a fence that went up behind it even higher and you couldn't tell if the ball went over the fence or stayed on top so they made a ground rule that said any ball that stayed on the scoreboard was a homerun," said Erskine."This ball that Thompson hit was a line drive. He hit the H and it stuck in plain view of everybody and he went to first and then he eased off and saw the ball was still there and Furillo was banging on the base of the scoreboard to try to dislodge it but it stayed up there. So he went to second then he went to third and then he scored. There was a big argument but the end result was they counted it a homerun. It never left the sight of the ballpark," Erskine laughed. "And then, before we could continue playing, they had to have the ground crew come out and remove the ball with a ladder so it wouldn't fall down during a game," Erskine added.

Andy Pafko was thought to be the final link to a championship club. He filled the left field slot that had been filled by platoon players for years. Although he only played

Erskine left signs name

part of 1951 and all of the 1952 season there, Pafko has fond memories of Ebbets Field. I always enjoyed playing in Ebbets Field. It was a hitter's park more or less like Wrigley Field," Pafko said. "The fans in Ebbets Field were just a little bit different. They were rabid. They loved their Dodgers. Hilda Chester, she was a character. That's why I said there were different individuals…just a bit different…it was an adventure every day at Ebbets Field," Pafko said.

"I enjoyed my career in Brooklyn but I was only there a year and a half before I was sold to the Milwaukee Braves. But I think playing with the Dodgers…I still believe it was the best ball club I ever played on. Man for man, position for position, we had great talent lead by Jackie Robinson and Pee Wee Reese and the whole gang. It was a great ball club," Pafko said. Pafko played a part in the "shot heard around the world" when Bobby Thompson wrecked the Dodgers pennant hope in 1951 with a ninth inning home run in the final playoff game in the Polo Grounds. He laughed when he said, "Yeah, a lot of people knew who threw the ball, a lot of people know who hit the ball but most people didn't know who was at the wall. It was yours truly," Pafko said. "When the ball hit the bat, I thought I had a shot at it. It was a line drive but instead of fading it took off and landed in the fourth or fifth row down the left field line (which was short in the Polo Grounds)," Pafko said."I think I would have got it in Brooklyn, no doubt about that but he hit it at the right time. The oddity of the whole story is we later became teammates with Milwaukee. And not only that, we became roommates!," Pafko said.

Bob Friend was a star pitcher for the Pittsburgh Pirates and he remembers a home run he hit at Ebbets Field. "I think I hit one off a pitcher by the name of Russ Meyer. He cussed me all around the bases too. That was what baseball was all about. You know the fans were so close to the field. They'd get 35,000 people in there and the place was packed. A night game at Ebbets Field was really something," said Friend. "Of course the ballpark was a tough park to pitch in. You know I think it was 335 down the left field line, 390 to center field and 280 to right field with that high fence. Of course Carl Furillo played it beautifully, you know the ricochets and every thing. It was a challenge to face that team in Ebbets Field," Friend said. "I had a pretty good record against the Dodgers in those years but I respected them. Facing Jackie Robinson…I think I remember the team as Billy Cox, Pee Wee Reese, Robinson

Gil Hodges, Roy Campanella, Andy Pafko, Duke Snider and Carl Furillo," Friend said of the Dodger lineup in the early fifties.

Gene Hermanski recalls a game "in 1947 at Ebbets Field, a night game we are at home of course. We're playing Pittsburgh and I'm playing in left field. Pete Reiser's playing in center field and Carl Furillo's in right field. Sometime during the game, I forget who the player was, (someone) hit a vicious ball into left center a little towards Pete where I couldn't reach it but he could," Hermanski said. "And that son of a gun, he (Reiser) reached for the ball, hit his head against the concrete and the ball trickled down between himself and the wall where the umpire couldn't see. The moment I got there, I got the ball and put it in his glove while waiting for someone (to help) but the umpire came out and called him (the batter) out," Hermanski chuckled. "He (Reiser) was hospitalized for quite a while after that. He was knocked out and right after that, maybe a month later, we had matted walls. At the time, they didn't know if he was going to live or die," said Hermanski.

Pitcher Ed Roebuck felt Ebbets Field was special. "The first time I went to Ebbets, it was a workout. I remember it was a cold that day and just walking out on the field it's like walking out in Yankee Stadium but I got the same feeling at Ebbets Field. You feel like you're in a traditional setting there. You just never forget. I think it had its own traditions just like Yankee Stadium did," Roebuck said. "It was one of the closest fields to the fans that I had ever been in or on. And it seems there was a relationship between the players and fans because they were so close to you. I wouldn't say it was always friendly but most of the time it was good fan reaction," said Roebuck. "Of all the different ballparks around that one was a real toughie to pitch in," noted Roebuck who led the Dodgers in saves in their championship year of 1955.

Ranson (Randy) Jackson played for and against the Dodgers at Ebbets Field. "Every time we (Chicago Cubs) would go into Ebbets Field we felt like the score was 2 or 3 to nothing before we started. It was the field, the fans and the make up of the team. They were proven winners and played confidently. Of course, as a Cub, we would usually end up at the bottom of the ladder but we did hold our own," said Jackson. "Getting traded to Brooklyn in 1956 completely changed my confidence. It's like osmosis-the winning tradition just wears on to you. It's great fun, in any sport, to be on top year after year. We were very wary of the fans as Cubs but they were our buddies as a Dodger. One of the fun parts of playing there was to watch the fans. The best word to use is inspirational," Jackson noted. "Playing with Brooklyn were probably the best professional years of my career. It was an honor and I very much respect the people who are still carrying the Brooklyn Dodger banner," said Jackson.

Bob Aspromonte was a 17 year old from Brooklyn's Lafayette High School when he signed a major league contract with the Dodgers. "Two days later, I was sitting down with Jackie Robinson

Variety of ads in left field

and Gil Hodges," he said. "Ebbets Field was always special. The most important thing was the closeness to the player. There was a relationship with the fans and everybody used to come out with shirts and ties. They were always dressed up coming to Ebbets Field," Aspromonte said.

Aspromonte's father and two brothers (who also played professional baseball) were all Like most Dodgers fans. "They could criticize the ball club but no one else could," he said Aspromonte also remembered, "They had the band that used to go around the stadium…always playing music. They would play everything and fire up the guys." Rather than just sit around as a bonus baby, Walter O'Malley had Aspromonte go to school and put him in the service with his son Peter. "I owe him a great deal of gratitude," Aspromonte said. When he got out of the service, he went to the minors and joined the team when they moved out west in Los Angeles. Catcher Andy Seminick who played on the Philadelphia Phillies and Cincinnati Reds from 1943 until 1957, recalls "it was always fun to play in Ebbets Field. The fans were great and well informed about the game. It was always a three hour game," Seminick said. "When Jackie Robinson came in, it seems like they all played better and he was a great player himself. They were great games when Robin Roberts (Phillie ace) and Don Newcombe would hook up," he added. "I played in the All Star game in 1949 (held at Ebbets Field) and Campanella took over and it was great," Seminick said. Although his Phillies defeated the Dodgers for the pennant in 1950, Seminick felt a little bit of envy. "The Dodgers seemed to always come up with the good ballplayers. It was a great organization Seems like every kid wanted to play for the Dodgers," he said.

Scoreboard Ebbets Field

Chapter 12   Hot Dog Stories

Humphrey Bogart was quoted once as saying, "A hotdog at the ballpark is better than a steak at the Ritz". There is a connection between hotdogs and baseball and the stories that connected them to Ebbets Field. Marcia Siegel has never gotten over first hot dog she had at Ebbets Field.

"My first memory of Ebbets Field was my dad and I going one Saturday in the middle of the summer. I must have been about seven or eight years old. My dad was a giant to me (all 5 ft 7 inches of him) and we walked up to seats that seemed as if we were going to heaven" Siegel said. "Then again anywhere with my dad was like going to heaven, I don't remember much of the game but boy did that hot dog taste stay with me. Hot dogs have never tasted as good since then," said Siegel. "I remember hanging out at Pete's hot dog stand (on McKeever Place) after the game and paying five cents for the hot dog (normally 10 cents) that was now slightly burnt on the griddle," Bob Gotdenker reveals. Inside Ebbets Field, "the caterer was Harry M. Stevens and I remember the hot dogs as good. They were served by a vendor with a contraption strapped to his back with warm water to keep them hot," Gotdenker said.

Twins & hot dogs

George Colligan was raised Catholic and this presented a problem at times. "Of course they (hotdogs) tasted much better on Friday! Especially since there was some question as to whether or not it was a mortal sin to eat them. Thinking about it today, of course one ponders the theology of a God who would send a kid to eternal damnation over an Ebbets Field hot dog," George Colligan said.

Barry Becher recalls "standing outside the ballpark at the hot dog stands and listening to the game and hearing 'Campanella fouls it over the roof' and all the kids running to capture the ball. If I got one, I would find out who hit a home run during the game and try to sell the ball after the game to a fan with a small child and tell them it was the home run ball. If I was lucky, I'd get three dollars and use that to get into the bleachers for five games (tickets were 60 cents to the bleachers)," Becher said.

"In 1950, I would get out of school at 3 pm and immediately run over to Ebbets to see if I could sneak into the game. The games started at 1 pm so we usually got in for free," he said. "When Rickey owned the team, the gates were usually unmanned after the 5th inning so it was easy. After O'Malley took over that policy ended and we had to be more creative to get into the games," Becher added.

Bums are champs

Stan Roth and his friends used to stand on the third base line waiting for foul balls near the hot dog stands on McKeever Place. "One of my best memories was when Joe Adcock hit a ball over the left field roof into the Sanitation Department parking lot on Montgomery Street," he said.

"When Adcock hit the ball and Red Barber announced it was going over the roof, about five of us ran up the street and started searching for the ball," Roth said. "A friend named Fred Gordon got the ball, took it into the park and got a Brave ball, an Adcock bat and $50 for it. I was told that the ball is now in the Hall of Fame but can't back that up," Roth said. Evidently, this must have been the day Adcock hit four homeruns at Ebbets Field. "Now let's swing around the corner onto Sullivan Place. There are windows high off the ground, windows with rounded tops, said to be those of the Dodger's clubhouse," said Jaykay (an alias for a fan who is in the witness protection program). "In warm weather these windows were always open. I confess to having joined others of my age and persuasion on more than one occasion before (and particularly after) games in standing beneath these windows and shouting words of praise, encouragement and, from time to time, vilification in the direction of our heroes," said Jaykay.

"One day, some older guy came along and said, 'That's not the locker room, you stupid kids. That's where they cook the hot dogs, Haw, Haw Haw'.

"I never followed up on this matter nor did I ever gather beneath those windows again, he said. "Now that I'm stable enough to handle to unvarnished truth, whatever it might be, I wish to know if in fact those were the clubhouse windows. I wonder if in fact Duke Snider might have heard my congratulations, if in fact my fervent pleas did not fall upon the deaf ears of somebody opening cartons of hotdog rolls," Jaykay said.

"We became friends with Nick 'The Greek' who had a hot dog stand on the third base side cross the street from the rotunda which was behind home plate, " Bil Phifer said. "As payment, for cleaning up around his stand after the crowds had gone into the ballpark, Nick would give us a soda, or on cold days, a hot chocolate and let us hang out and listen to the game on his radio. That gave us the edge," Phifer said. "Instead of standing there looking up towards the roof waiting for a ball to appear (and not know what was going on), we waited for Red Barber or Connie Desmond (Dodger announcers) to tell us when there was a foul ball on the roof and which direction it was coming," he said. "This enabled us to get close enough to the area to catch it on the fly or, at worse, on the first bounce. That not only increased the quantity but also the quality of our baseballs,' Phifer said.

Lysa Yitzk recalls Ebbets Field a little differently than most people. "It might sound crazy but the first thought I have is the hot dog vendors in the stands with that Guildens mustard," Yitzk said.

Harvey Kornberg had a favorite place to get free baseballs outside Ebbets Field. "On days and nights when we could not get in, we would hang around near one of the hot dog stands that were in front of the rotunda and listened to the game on the radio at the stand," he said. "When we heard Red Barber call a foul ball, we all got ready. Red was terrific-he ALWAYS stated where the foul was going: 'Foul ball third base side'," he said. "I later learned that he did this on purpose for us kids. One year (my best year) I got seven foul balls," said Kornberg. "The scramble was amazing, picture about a dozen kids going after a ball after it had bounced (I never saw anyone catch a foul on the fly as it came over). We were usually pretty fair about it. Whoever emerged from the scrum with the ball could be sure it was his," Kornberg added.

Bob Karasik actually sold hot dogs at Ebbets Field with a friend as a joke "for a short time and I got fired. I was the worst salesman in the entire company. It was a company called the Harry M. Stevens and they had the franchise for 30 or 40 years," he said. Karasik got canned because, "I would spend my time watching the games" instead of selling hot dogs.

Many natives called those hot dogs "dirty water hot dogs" because they were cooked in the same water over and over again. Karasik also mentioned that the hot dogs were not cooked in beer (like many thought) because it would be "way too expensive". "They were as cheap as you could get. They would use the water over and over again. They just wanted to get (hot dogs) them out…they were terrible," Karasik said.

Dorothy Zaremba had a dad who possessed one of the most desired things in Brooklyn. "My dad had a press pass to Ebbets Field that allowed him and a guest to enter all of the Dodger home games played during the season. Very frequently, an older friend of mine, Richie Levy would take me to the ballgames at Ebbets Field and we used Dad's Brooklyn Eagle Pass to get into the park, "she said. "Richie was about 16 years old and his dad owned a candy store. It was one of those old time candy stores with the marble counters and swivel red seats. Rickie would pack up a bag of goodies from his Dad's store for us to eat during the game and I would get us into the game with the free passes. It was sort of a tradeoff and my parents trusted that I was in good hands with Richie and I was," Zaremba said.

"Richie and I would start out seated in the bleachers and as the game progressed, we worked our way closer and closer to the field boxes. We learned to coax older gents to buy us hotdogs and a soda by telling them that we left our money at home. We had to make sure that we did not pick one of the regulars to buy our hotdogs as many of them got to know us," Dorothy Zaremba said.

"It had to be 1954 or 1955 when I was just a young chubby girl who wanted so much to watch the Brooklyn Dodgers every opportunity I could get. No matter how I got to Ebbets Field, it didn't matter just as long as I was there…I had it all," she said.

"I have so many memories of my "tomboy" baseball youth. I even traded that much sought after Mickey Mantle card for three Dodgers Topps cards. I now realize it was a dumb trade but if you are a true Dodger fan no Mickey Mantle card, rookie or not, is worth more than any Dodger card," Zaremba said. "Yes I wonder where Richie is today, the candy store is gone, Dad is gone and so are the Dodgers from Brooklyn. Gee, did I love my youth and those Brooklyn Dodgers," she said.

Zaremba and her husband left Brooklyn on Oct. 15, 2001. They now live in a retirement village in the Pinelands of New Jersey. Believe it or not, they now root for the New York Yankees.

Chapter 13   This Is Next Year

Spring training in 1955 started with the usual grumbling of players and one who claimed, "We'll win it in spite of him (Alston)". Jackie Robinson called Walter Alston a "wooden Indian" and even announcer Vin Scully noted, "He should have been born in another time period; he would have been comfortable back in the days of the old west riding shotgun on a stagecoach."

Instead, Walter Alston road herd on his Dodgers in his second year at the helm. When his authority was challenged he would often remark, "We can talk. We can talk right here, right now, or you and I can go outside and talk." Standing an impressive 6 foot 2 inches and weighing 195 pounds, no one took him up on the offer.

Of course, winning had a way soothing everyone's nerves and the Dodgers did plenty of that to start the 1955 season. They began with a 22-2 record and never looked back. Ed Roebuck was a rookie in 1955 and he noted "my record doesn't show it but I lead that club in saves and I did it all in the first half of the season." "Of all the different ballparks around, that one (Ebbets Field) was a real toughie to pitch in.

First base Side

Russ Meyer (fellow pitcher) told me once that 'The home plate was higher than the top of the left field fence,'" Roebuck said. "That was 348 feet (from home plate)…and a little bit of an unreliable number. Can you imagine Mantle, Mays, Snider and those guys hitting in that park? Center field was what…367 feet? When it was first built they didn't have seats out there so they kept adding seats." Roebuck's first appearance came in relief of Carl Erskine. "I had pitched for Alston at Montreal for three or four years and the first game he brought me into was in Philly," Roebuck said. "Carl (Erskine) was pitching and had let in four or five runs. For some reason he got wild and loaded the bases and had a count on a hitter. Walt brought me in (I was warming up with Clem Labine) and I thought 'wow'. I thought he was going to bring in Labine not me. I thought if he has enough confidence in me then I have enough confidence to do my best and I got out of the inning," Roebuck laughed.

In the middle of August, with the Dodgers 13 games ahead of Milwaukee, O'Malley reiterated his intention to move out of New York if a new stadium was not built by 1958 in a meeting with New York Mayor Robert F. Wagner. He also mentioned that the New York Giants would probably follow them. O'Malley noted that since the largest revenue of each club came from the 22 games between each other it just made sense. He said the Giants drew 344.674 fans in their 11 games against the Dodgers that year and it represented more than 40% of their total attendance.

"I don't want to think about the Dodgers getting out of Brooklyn until I'm convinced we can't get a new ball field," O'Malley said after his downtown ballpark proposal at Flatbush and Atlantic Avenue was shot down by Robert Moses the construction coordinator of New York City. But without a centrally located site, where the club could build its own park, and without a municipal stadium to lease, the club would probably have to move out of Brooklyn after the 1957 season the Dodger owner added.

Moses offered a site in the Flushing Meadows area of Queens (where the World's Fair had been held) but O'Malley didn't want to build on swamp land besides he said "They're not the Brooklyn

Dodgers if they're not on Brooklyn." O'Malley put pressure on city officials by announcing the Dodgers would play 7 "home" games at Roosevelt Stadium in Jersey City, New Jersey in 1956 and 1957.

Back on the field, Roy Campanella was having his third MVP season with 32 homers and 107 RBIs and deft handling of an ordinary pitching staff after Don Newcombe. Newcombe won 20 games and lead the Dodgers to clinching the National League pennant on September 8. Once again the Yankees would be their series opponent and the odds makers picked them as 6-7 favorites.

The World Series opened at Yankee Stadium and three home runs (two by Joe Collins and one from Elston Howard) finished off the Dodgers 6-5 in front of 63,869 fans. The Dodgers who lead the majors with 201 homers replied with single shots from Carl Furillo and Duke Snider but it wasn't enough. Jackie Robinson tried to fire up his mates with a steal of home in the eight inning but it didn't change the outcome. Newcombe lost his third series game and Whitey Ford improved his record to 2-1.

Game 2 saw the Yankees score four runs in the fourth inning to take a commanding 2-0 lead the 1955 World Series. Yankee pitcher Tommy Byrne, 35 and considered washed up before the season, went the distance and was the first lefty to do it against the Dodgers in over a year. He even knocked in two runs in the fateful fourth inning.

The Subway Series switched back to Brooklyn and things looked bleak for the Dodgers. No team had ever come back to win a Series after losing the first two games. On top of that the Dodgers had a 52 year jinx of never winning a world championship. Even Yankee manager Casey Stengel got in the act by posing with a broom to suggest that a possible four game sweep was in the offing.

Walter Alston chose lefty Johnny Podres over Carl Erskine to face the surging Yankees in Game 3. It was Podres' 23rd birthday as he and 34,209 Dodgers fans celebrated with a 8-3 complete game victory over the Yankees. Podres felt vindicated by Alston's confidence in putting him on the World Series roster. After a 9-10 injury filled season, Podres salvaged his spot with two scoreless innings in the final regular season game against Pittsburgh "I never had a better assortment of stuff. The change up was my best pitch. I usually throw it only four or five times a game but yesterday when I found out early that I could get it over, I relied on it all afternoon. I guess I showed 'em I could go nine innings They keep saying I can't go nine innings. That makes me mad. I didn't feel tired once today," Podres said.

Game 4 saw Carl Erskine start but he didn't last through the fourth inning as the Yankees built a 3-1 lead. Roy Campanella and Gil Hodges each belted homeruns in the Dodger fourth and Duke Snider added one in the fifth inning to add six runs for a 7-3 lead that was not headed. Clem Labine held off the Yanks and Brooklyn won 8-5 with fourteen hits off five Yankee hurlers.

Game 5 saw both teams scrambling for a starter. Don Newcombe had a stiff arm and was unavailable so Alston picked 6-4, 178 pound rookie Roger Craig. Yankee manager Stengel who noted "pitching is our trouble" opted for Bob Grim. Duke Snider hit two home runs to help give the Dodgers a 5-3 win and the Series lead in front of 36,796 fans (the largest crowd to ever see a World Series game in Ebbets Field). Helping the Dodger cause were injuries to Yankee outfielders Mickey Mantle and Hank Bauer as the Bronx Bombers could only muster six hits. "Bauer told me he couldn't make it," Stengel said. "Mantle's no better today than he was yesterday. If a fellow can't run and can't hit, he's no good to you. It's tough playing on one leg," Stengel added. The Series shifted back to Yankee Stadium and the mood had shifted in the Dodger locker room. They felt they had their foes on the ropes. Dodger manager Walter Alston said, "This is a different year and a different Dodger team". On the other hand, Yankee manager Casey Stengel was in a foul mood as he grumbled," I'm not predicting anything except it will go seven." He did admit to being stunned after losing three straight at Ebbets Field. "We should have won here," Stengel said. "We won here before and have only ourselves to blame. I'll be glad to get back to the open range in our park but that park is no excuse. It's more us. We didn't take advantage of the short fences. I got the guys to hit homers too. Maybe more than they have. They just didn't hit as many as Brooklyn did," Stengel said.

Whitey Ford faced Karl Spooner in Game 6 and the contest was decided in the first inning. The Yankees scored five times and were propelled by Bill Skowron's two run homer and chased Spooner out of the game and baseball too (he never pitched another major league game). Ford handcuffed the Dodgers on four hits and only allowed a fourth inning run as he defeated them 5-1 for his second Series win in 1955.

Game 7 now approached and the Dodger's best pitcher was still unavailable. Don Newcombe had stiffness in his shoulder since his first game loss. "It's still sore," he said. "I didn't even bother to throw today because of the pain." Alston already had his mind made up earlier when he said before Game 6, "If there is a seventh game, Johnny Podres will pitch Tuesday."

Game 7 was a pitcher's duel between Podres and Tommy Byrne. Gil Hodges knocked in two runs with a single in the fourth inning and a sacrifice fly in the sixth. The Yankees best chance to score came in the bottom of the sixth inning. Yankee second baseman Billy Martin had walked and Gil McDougald got a bunt single when Yogi Berra hit an opposite field drive toward the left field foul pole. It appeared to be an extra base and game tying hit as it sailed deep into left field but defensive replacement Sandy Amoros snagged the ball with an outstretched glove after racing from his position in left center field to almost falling in the stands in the corner by the foul pole. Amoros then fired to cutoff man Pee Wee Reese and he in turn threw to first baseman Hodges to double off McDougald. The Yankees last big threat had been crushed. Podres kept them off balance again with his change ups and he shut them out 2-0.

Inside Ebbets Field

The Dodgers were FINALLY World Champions for the first time at 3:43 pm on October 5th, 1955. New York City then experienced the greatest number of phone calls since V-J day. There were 226,866 phone calls on the day of Game 7. A person trying to make a business call got no dial tone.

The Daily News sold an extra 125,000 copies with cartoonist Leo O'Mealia's version of the Brooklyn bum gracing the front page with WHO'S A BUM as the headline. Bedlam broke out in Brooklyn.

"On the trip back on the bus from Yankee Stadium to Brooklyn," recalled Snider in Harvey Frommer's New York City Baseball, "everyone must have known our route." "Everyone had a sign and the streets were packed with people making noise. I'll never forget it. We had the greatest fans in the world. They lived and died with us and this was their moment," continued Snider People shot off firecrackers, banged pots and pans, yelled, cheered and made as much noise as possible throughout the

Borough of Churches. Fans rode around in automobiles honking their horns and much liquor flowed. For many, it truly was a dream come true. The underdog Dodgers, the David's had slayed the mighty baseball Goliath's from the Bronx. Schools and many businesses closed the next day for the championship parade. Dennis Desmond went out "in the street to be with my friends. I was just 11 and I just wanted to yell and celebrate with my friends. Every house had a radio or TV tuned to all the games anyway and everyone was in a joyous mood. It was fun to see the whole neighborhood and the Borough having so much fun," Desmond said.

"I was 14 years old when they won," said Barry Becher. "I played the trumpet back then and was pretty good. I went over to Ebbets Field that night and made a ton of noise with all the other celebrants. Some guy had a convertible and he insisted that I sit in the back on top of his folded convertible top and I blew that horn until the wee hours while circling Ebbets!" Becher said. "It was GREAT".

"My father, photographer Robert Olen, was furious at me for my happiness when the Dodgers finally won their first World Series because he was working for the Yankees and this Yankee loss was going to cost him $$$$$," said Dodger fan Ivan Danzig.

"In 1955, I was attending James Madison High School which was about 2 miles from Ebbets," Grace Lichtenstein recalled. "My final class of the day was girl's gym. There must have been 40 of us all seated in the center of the gym, crowded around one transistor radio, listening with our hearts in our mouths to the final three outs. When they last out was made, we were all yelling and screaming and crying. And since the gym was in a wing of the school that stuck out beyond the classrooms, we could hear the entire school cheering through the windows. Horns began to honk in the streets as drivers celebrated. The whole borough of Brooklyn seemed to erupt," Lichtenstein said. "I don't remember anything of how I got home that day or how many people I hugged. What I hold in my heart today, so many years later, is a feeling of joy and relief, mixed with a touch of bittersweetness -not so much because they moved away, but because two months earlier, my paternal grandfather, who was the motivating force behind my love of baseball and who lived with my family, had passed away. He had spent 85 years on earth, most of them in Brooklyn, and alas, never lived to see the team finally capture the World Series," she said. "One appropriate touch, however; my grandfather died in his favorite easy chair, cigar in hand, watching a Dodger game on the family TV," Lichtenstein fondly remembers.

Ever the party pooper, Walter O'Malley brought up the new stadium problem even while the Flatbush faithful danced in the streets. "Right now the matter is pretty much out of our hands," he said. "But I don't see how anyone could want to see the Dodgers leave Brooklyn. Certainly, we don't want to go anywhere else and I am now more confident then ever that something will turn up which will enable us to build a new home befitting the World Champions," O'Malley declared.

Ebbets Field was doomed but was Brooklyn too?

Chapter 14   The Last Years

The Dodgers were a confident club heading into the 1956 season. Hot on their trail were the young Milwaukee Braves who had a power hitting righty-lefty combination of Joe Adcock and Eddie Mathews that terrorized the league. Adcock had a habit of tattooing Dodger pitching. He hit four homeruns and a double in one game at Ebbets Field in 1954. His 18 total bases set a Major League record to earn their respect and occasional bean balls. The very next day, he was taken off the field after being hit in the head. Fortunately he was wearing a plastic shield inside his helmet (one of the first) which probably saved him from a fractured skull. Adding to the Braves potent offense was relative newcomer Hank Aaron. Aaron in his third season lead the league with a .328 average. He also led the league with 200 hits and 34 doubles in 1956.

Fan John Tiernan still has vivid memories of the beginning of the 1956 season. "A year after Brooklyn won the World Series, Lincoln Savings Bank sponsored a parade down Flatbush Ave. to Ebbets Field to honor the '55 Dodgers. My brother and I somehow got invited to participate with a group of other kids and were invited to the opening game," Tiernan said. "Before the game started, we met in some auditorium with all the players and coaches. We all got to ask one question and the one who asked the best question got $5 (everyone else got $1 to buy a hot dog at the game). Every player was gracious and answered a lot of stupid "kid" questions. My brother won the $5 by asking Johnny Podres what he was thinking of on the last pitch of the game. He said he was just hoping to get him out," Tiernan said. "Each of us received an autographed baseball of all the Dodgers from the '55 World Series and got to see the opening game at Ebbets Field. It was a beautiful day with the sun shining and the grass seemed more green than any I've ever seen," he said.

Braves Eddie Mathews at third base

The Dodgers trailed the Braves most of the season and the chase brought out an extra 166,000 fans to Ebbets Field from the previous year's total. Don Newcombe had his finest year with a 27-7 record and richly deserved the Cy Young and MVP awards. He paced the staff but without the help of a former hated rival, the Bums never would had caught the Braves.

Sal (the Barber) Maglie was thought to be finished when the Giants waived him in the middle of the '55 season. Cleveland picked him up with little results and pawned him off on the Dodgers in May of '56. Maglie had earned his reputation shaving batter's chins when they crouched close to the plate and many of those batters had been Dodgers. Brooklyn fans were initially as shocked as Giant fans when Leo Durocher switched allegiances nine years before. Carl Furillo and Jackie Robinson posed for photos with Maglie to reassure fans the world had not turned upside down. Still, they had to wonder if he had anything left in his arm. However, Maglie won them over with an outstanding 13-5 mark and the lowest ERA on the pitching staff. His clutch hurling over the final week with a no hitter over Philadelphia and win over Pittsburgh put the Dodgers in front to stay. They won the pennant by one game. Henry Becker was there on Saturday September 29, "when after a Friday night rainout, my dad and I, along with a friend of my dad's and his son, went all the way to Ebbets Field from our home in New Jersey (it was a long trip then) to see the Dodgers beat the Pirates in a double header. "The Braves lost that night vaulting the Dodgers into a one game lead which they preserved the next day to win their last pennant in Brooklyn," said Becker.

President Eisenhower at 1st World Series game 1956

The 1956 World Series started out with President Dwight Eisenhower throwing out the first ball and 39 yr old Maglie took over from there by striking out ten Yankees and only giving up nine hits in a 6-3 Dodger victory at Ebbets Field. Gil Hodges and Jackie Robinson each hit homeruns off Whitey Ford who seemed jinxed in Brooklyn. Before the game, Ford mentioned that "They say left-handers never win at Ebbets Field. I'd like to disprove that." He only lasted three innings and was charged with the loss. Maglie, in contrast, was ecstatic with his performance. "This was my greatest thrill. Yes, even more of a thrill than my no-hitter," he said. "They claim you can't have everything you want in life but believe me with this series victory I have close to all I ever wished for," Maglie continued.

Game 2 was a marathon slugfest that almost lasted 3 ½ hours. The Daily News called it "Murder At Ebbets Field" as the Dodgers roughed up seven Yankee pitchers for a 13-8 drubbing. Oddly enough, the Yankees were "bombing" Newcombe in the first two innings when they scored six runs (four of them courtesy of a Yogi Berra grand slam). Things turned around quickly when the Dodgers jumped all over Don Larsen for six runs of their own in the bottom of the second. Brooklyn pitchers Ed Roebuck and Don Bessent cooled off the Yankees and only allowed them 2 more runs while fellow Dodger hitters were just getting warmed up. They scored five more runs in the next three innings and two more in the eighth. Many fans must have wondered, "After waiting so many years for a championship, could a second one come so easily?" Even Captain Pee Wee Reese chimed in, "That was a big lift when we did it last year. We found out we could beat 'em and why shouldn't we do it again," he said. The answer would come with the next three games at Yankee Stadium. It wouldn't be easy at all.

Pitcher Clem Labine (crewcut) mingles with fans

Whitey Ford regained his composure and pitched a complete game in Game 3 at the spacious House that Ruth Built. Billy Martin hit a second inning homer and former Cardinal Enos Slaughter added a three run homer in the 6th inning to power the Yanks to a 5-3 victory.

Game 4 saw another complete game victory by Yankee pitcher Tom Sturdivant as Mickey Mantle and Hank Bauer hit round trippers in a 6-2 Series tying game. Sal Maglie started Game 5 and he was superb in only allowing five hits and two runs but Don Larsen was absolutely perfect for the Bronx Bombers. Larsen was 11-5 in the regular season and named by Ted Williams as one of the toughest pitchers in the American League but he had been roughed up in Game 2 and just two years before had lost 21 games while hurling for the St. Louis Browns. Mickey Mantle provided all the support Larsen needed with a 4th inning homerun and a great running circus catch in deep left center off a smash from the bat of Gil Hodges in the 5th inning as the Yankees won 2-0. Don Larsen shut down the power laden Dodgers with a no windup delivery that seemed to throw off the Bums. The crowd of 64,619 cheered every out from the 7th inning on. No one had ever pitched a no run, no hit, perfect World Series game before but Larsen did it and gave the Yankees the Series lead.

Facing elimination back at Ebbets Field, Dodger pitcher Clem Labine befuddled the New Yorkers for ten innings and shut them out 1-0. Jackie Robinson's left field liner over Enos Slaughter's head knocked in Junior Gilliam for the only run of the game. Labine has noted that his shutout before Bobby Thompson's 1951 Game 3 playoff homerun (Shot Heard 'round the World) and his 1956 shutout (after Larsen's perfect game) "are two of the most forgotten games ever pitched". Labine only allowed four hits and evened the Series for the staggering Dodgers. Of course, Dodger fans would argue otherwise as the shutout put them in position to win their second championship. Before the Series started, Dodger Captain Pee Wee Reese noted that "This is the same team that did it, except for Johnny Podres. We could use Johnny again this year." Podres, of course, was in the service and unavailable. However Don Newcombe was there. Unfortunately, Newcombe's arm was just about to fall off after a fantastic season.

Locker room after last game Sept. 24, 1957

Yogi Berrra hit a home run in the first inning and the third inning of Game 7 to send Newk to the showers and the Yankees on their way to a 9-0 wipeout of the Dodgers.

The power laden Dodger lineup blew a fuse and batted .195 for the Series. They also were shutout in two of the last three games and only scored one run in the last 28 innings they played. It was an inglorious end for Newcombe who had been trying to shake off a "choker" image hung on him for his past Series failures. He left the park early after getting knocked out and after visiting his parents and wife left overnight and "his whereabouts were unknown". He showed up the next day for a team flight to Japan for a goodwill tour but personal problems were starting to mount for him and his career was downhill from there.

This was also the last World Series game ever played in Ebbets Field and 33,782 fans went home disappointed. Jackie Robinson had also played his last game and things would never be quite the same for the Dodger faithful. In late October, O'Malley sold Ebbets Field for $3 million to real estate developer Marvin Kratter. He envisioned a high rise, middle income housing at Sullivan and McKeever . The Dodgers took out a three year lease (with a two year option) to cover them while they worked on getting a new stadium.

Meanwhile, only $25,000 was spared for an engineering and economic survey for a new stadium by the Sports Center Authority. Getting the Dodgers a new home didn't seem to be a high priority for city officials.

On December 13th, Robinson was traded to the New York Giants for journeyman pitcher Dick Littlefield and $30,000. The heart and soul of six pennant winners in ten seasons, Robinson was now graying and considerably slower on the base paths. Robinson at first was stunned. "Naturally, I'm disappointed to leave Brooklyn," he said. Asked if he would retire, Robinson said he'd need a few days to get away and think it over.

Jackie Robinson didn't announce his retirement until January 1957 when he wrote an article in Look magazine called "Why I'm Quitting Baseball" for $50,000. Also in January, O'Malley hired Ringling Brother's clown Emmet Kelly to entertain fans at Ebbets Field in 1957. Kelly whose character seemed the perfect looking Bum envisioned by cartoonist Willard Mullin was hired by O'Malley to help ease the "tension" at Ebbets Field and Big "OM" thought this would help.

Dave Anderson, who covered the Dodgers for the Brooklyn Eagle in the early 50's, had his suspicions like many others about what was going to happen. "All along …it always seemed to me that from at least 1955 that everyone knew he (O'Malley) was going to L.A. one way or another. You know he kept saying 'Well, I want a stadium here in Brooklyn' …and then they (politicians) said 'We'll give you this land out near the World's Fair' (which is the land where Shea Stadium is today he said 'Oh, I couldn't take the Brooklyn Dodgers to Queens' so he took them to L.A.," Anderson said. "You never felt Walter O'Malley was on the level," he said.

Stan Isaacs, who also covered the Dodgers in those days, thought like many others that "O'Malley was bluffing." As far as the changing demographics were concerned around the ballpark as a reason for moving, Isaacs has strong feelings about that. "It was racist, subtle racist talk that the borough was becoming black and what was the long range future …and (he) fed them (the press) stories like people were urinating on the runways, which knowing O'Malley was a question of whether it was true," he said.

However, Isaacs like many others, was still surprised when the Dodgers left. "You know it was because he said his roots were in Brooklyn, so we believed him," Isaacs remarked.

Others didn't need much convincing that Ebbets Field had to go. "Ebbets Field had too few rest rooms, overcrowded concessions, inadequate parking, and from a business man's point of view, a profit-limiting seating capacity," according to Christopher Jennison in his book Wait Till Next Year. "And it was, in the final analysis, a business consideration that transferred the Dodgers to Los Angeles and sentenced the rickety old park at the corner of Bedford and Sullivan to demolition," said Jennison.

Fresco Thompson is his book Every Diamond Doesn't Sparkle mentioned that the Brooklyn ball yard had seen better days. "It wasn't just one girder rotting on Ebbets Field-it was all of them. Yearly maintenance was mounting, running to astronomical figures of from two hundred and fifty to three hundred thousand dollars annually," he said.

Robert Creamer in Steve Delsohn's True Blue noted," The grand stands were dirty and smelled of stale beer. The clubhouse was so small and cluttered, even the Dodger clubhouse, it was like someone's attic. And the visiting clubhouse was worse. It was like the Black Hole of Calcutta. This was a decrepit, antiquated old ballpark that just could not continue. That's all there was to it. They had to have a change," he continued.

Although many thought Ebbets Field was falling apart in later years, long time ticket taker Joe McDonald didn't notice it. "He (O'Malley) didn't spend a lot of money improving it but I didn't detect that it was committed to run down…it remained a romantic spot in my heart," McDonald said. Of course, just because it made sense it didn't make it right. Sixty eight years of Brooklyn fan loyalty didn't mean a thing. The last 13 years, they came out over a million plus each year to root their hometown Dodgers on. They had made the Dodgers the richest team in the National League for years. Moving out of Ebbets Field was one thing but moving completely out of Brooklyn was another. Most thought something would happen to keep them in the borough.

However other things were falling into place for O'Malley in February, when he was able to swap minor league franchises with the Cub's Phillip Wrigley and gain territorial rights in the Los Angeles area at an owner's dinner. Wrigley had been feuding with Los Angeles officials and was glad to unload his minor league park and team for the Dodger's Fort Worth, Texas affiliation.

The stage was now set for Walter O'Malley's treacherous abandonment of Brooklyn Dodger fans. He purchased a 44 seat Convair airplane for $775.000 and made several trips out west to met with Mayor Norris Poulson. He traded a 20,000 seat L. A. minor league ball park (Wrigley Field) for the Chavez Ravine site where he would build a 50,000 seat stadium with plenty of parking over 300 acres.

On May 11, two weeks before the National League owners approved the franchise switch for the Giants and Dodgers, the New York Post reported that Walter O'Malley told L.A. officials that the Dodgers would play their home games at the L.A. Coliseum in 1958. National League owners told the Dodgers and Giants on May 28 to make up their minds by October 1 if they were going to move. Cincinnati was rumored to be interested in moving into Brooklyn but fans wanted their Bums to stay put. Civic groups were formed to keep the Dodgers in Brooklyn but marches, petitions and letters to the editor didn't convince city officials to cave into O'Malley's plans.

New York Mayor Robert Wagner vowed to "do everything I can to keep the Dodgers and Giants in New York". But it was too late. Time for talk was long past. O'Malley had convinced Giant's owner Horace Stoneham that they should take advantage of a second gold rush out west. A Pay -per -view TV scheme was a plum O'Malley dangled in front of Stoneham as part of their devil's pact. The two team's rivalry could continue between Los Angeles and San Francisco plus they could enjoy greater riches than possible in New York.

Stoneham didn't take too much convincing and he abandoned his first thought of moving to his minor league city of Minneapolis which already had a stadium in place. Stoneham formally told Baseball Commissioner Ford Frick on Oct.1 the Giants were going to San Francisco.

O'Malley got a deadline extension for announcing his move and kept playing a cat and mouse game with New York and Los Angeles officials to get the best deal possible. On Oct. 8, a brief announcement noted that "the stockholders and directors of the Brooklyn Baseball Club have today met and unanimously agreed that necessary steps be taken to draft the Los Angeles territory."

Brooklyn Borough President John Cashmore said "I have personally done everything I could to keep the Dodgers in Brooklyn but I couldn't do it alone." He also mentioned he would "leave nothing undone to have National League baseball continued in Brooklyn. It is important to the economic life of the borough."

In their last season, 1,028,258 fans came out to cheer their Brooklyn Dodgers at Ebbets Field in spite of every home game being televised, countless freebies being distributed and O'Malley's constant threat to leave if he didn't get what he wanted.

There were a few memorable dates at Ebbets Field in 1957 such as the D-Day fog out. On June 6, a fog stirred up by a storm in the Atlantic Ocean came ashore and postponed a game after a one hour and 26 minute delay during the Dodgers half of the first inning. It was the only major league game ever called because of fog.

On July 19, between a twi-night double header, 28,724 fans cheered as Gil Hodges was given an Appreciation Night where he received everything from a new convertible to dill pickles. The Dodgers took both games from the Chicago Cubs and Hodges got 1,000th RBI of his career.

September 24, was the last game at Ebbets Field and only 6,702 fans attended the wake-like proceedings. Dodgers Johnny Podres, Carl Erskine, and Sandy Koufax had their picture taken singing Auld Lang Syne after their 2-0 victory over the Pittsburgh Pirates . Organist Gladys Goodding played apropos songs like "Thanks for The Memories," "Don't Ask Me Why I'm Leaving," "How Can You Say We're Through" among other tunes during the game.

Roy Campanella hosted a beer and crab fingers "farewell' party for the players which the writers and broadcasters joined in after the game. Park employees had a few toasts afterwards under the stands as well while a few fans were seen crying. Charlie Ebbets, who fought to keep the team in Brooklyn so many years before, must have rolled over in his grave when the Brooklyn fans became disenfranchised. His field had become outdated and was soon to be abandoned but it still had a few more years of life left.

Chapter 15   Fans and Ballpark Abandoned

When the Dodgers left Brooklyn for Los Angeles, the fans felt like children of divorcing parents. The "adults" (state, city and borough authorities and Walter O'Malley) had been squabbling for years about a new stadium and where its location should be. Having the Dodgers play seven "home" games in New Jersey during the 1956 and 1957 season was O'Malley's way of getting official's attention that he might move further away if they didn't see things his way.

Ebbets Field 1958

Robert Moses the building czar of bridges and roads in New York was arguably the most influential and powerful man in government at the time and he didn't want O'Malley's ball park in downtown Brooklyn. Too much traffic congestion he thought. It was to be built in Flushing Meadows, Queens or no where else according to Moses. As time was running out, Nelson Rockefeller tried to put together a group to buy the Dodgers. Clothier Abe Stark, of Ebbets Field HIT SIGN, WIN SUIT billboard fame and later Borough President, even offered a plan to build a ball yard at Prospect Park in Brooklyn. O'Malley and Moses would not budge.

Finally, O'Malley turned away from the aging Ebbets Field and the Brooklyn family that had been so faithful for so many years and he left for glamorous Los Angeles where movie stars and a pot of gold at the end of the rainbow could be found.

Ebbets Field was on life support and abandoned by the team it was built for. However the last two years that Ebbets Field existed was checkered with a variety of events held there and some fans still remember them

Dodger fan Charles Hefferman went to Ebbets Field after his hometown heroes left for California after the 1957 season. "The last time I was in Ebbets Field was May, 1958 the first year the team was in L.A. I went there to see the championship game in the Public School Athletic League. Friends of ours were on one team," said Hefferman. "As I entered the stands, I immediately noticed how the park was unpainted and not maintained. It was strange to be able to sit wherever you wanted, with no ushers. As I took my seat behind what had been the Dodger dugout, and looked around the park, the depressing reality sunk in that they were really gone. I was 14 years old and I think I grew up that day," Hefferman said.

"When the Dodgers left after the '57 season, we Ebbets Field kids were crushed- I mean CRUSHED! Nothing was the same after that," Harvey Kornberg said.

"When the Dodgers found it necessary to leave Brooklyn, I felt then and still do that New York had started the decline," said David Bray.

"Oh how I loved Ebbets Field and our Dodgers. I cried when they left," Dennis Desmond recalled. "I went to the 'Let's Keep The Dodgers in Brooklyn rally at Borough Hall. It was my first great disappointment in life, but not my last," said Desmond

Alan Greenberg was in disbelief when he heard the Dodgers were moving to Los Angeles. "How could anyone go to California? It was so far away…and for money no less! Remember that the final decision to move both the Dodgers and the Giants didn't come until after the season ended so people didn't take it too seriously during the year and there was no rush for souvenirs at the last game," said Greenberg.

"From the war years to 1955, I was one of 'the faithful' rooting to my hearts content and at the end of the season seeing the picture of the BUM on the back page of the Daily News with the caption 'Wait 'til next year', which we all did," Jack Skelly said.

"Then in 1955 I went into the army and went to Germany and did not have the joy of celebrating when the Dodgers finally beat the Yanks. When I came home in 1957, the team left me high and dry and went to La La land. Needless to say I was crushed with the rest of 'the faithful'," said Skelly. Brian Strum knows why the Brooklyn fans felt deserted. "The Dodger fans were, if not adoringly supportive, at least loyal during the thirties. Yes, they suffered, and did not idolize the players, as they would 20 years later. But Babe Herman's being hit on the head by a fly ball, and three Dodgers on one base were laughingly 'theirs'. The Dodgers were their team because they were from Brooklyn, which was home," he said. "Going to Manhattan or the Bronx was like going to another town-foreign, far way, not hometown," Strum noted. "And maybe they were loyal because this team was the only thing these people had. Broadway, Wall Street etc. was across the river. Brooklyn's downtown was topped by Times Square and Herald Square and Prospect Park was topped by Central Park and the Bronx Zoo. Aside from Coney Island, what else could the population hold dear as their own? The Dodgers gave these people identity, enhanced and embellished by media, an identity one could relate to, and loyal to—not perfect, not dominant but something close to family and friends, with faults and blemishes, and close to real life," Strum added.

It was bad enough when the hometown paper the Brooklyn Eagle folded in early 1955 and then the Trolley cars ceased to operate but this was a disaster.

Brooklyn Dodgers fan Robert Smith summed it up. "We cried when they did and laughed when they did but nothing can cure the hurt of my BROOKLYN BUMS leaving town. I still root for the Dodgers but not in the same way. Sometimes, I still sit in front of the TV looking at a Dodger crowd and thinking 'If they only knew what it was like being a real BROOKLYN DODGER FAN'," Smith said.

Branch Rickey voiced what a great majority of baseball fan's felt when he said," It was a crime against a community of 3,000,000 to move the Dodgers. Not

End is near

that the move was unlawful, since people have the right to do as they please with their property. But a baseball club in any city in America is a quasi-public institution and in Brooklyn the Dodgers were public without the quasi. Not even a succeeding generation will forget or forgive the removal of its Dodger team".

On May 25, 1958, the Scottish soccer champions Hearts of Midlothian defeated Manchester City 6-5 in an exhibition game in front of 20,606 rain drenched fans. Jimmy Wardaugh scored three goals for the Scottish team. On July 14, 1959, Bill Shea, chairman of the N. Y. baseball committee, said it would take no more than 14 months to complete a new stadium but "even if it took a little longer, we always could use Ebbets Field for a month or two. " St. John's University played three of their baseball games there in 1959. A demolition derby was the last event that took place there and it completely tore up the sod and left the former shrine to the Dodgers a complete mess.

The end finally came on a Tuesday, February 23, 1960. Only 200 or so freezing fans attended as former Dodger broadcaster Al Helfer acted as the master of ceremonies as demolition of Ebbets Field began. The demolition of 47 year old Ebbets Field would take 10 months. The site would be replaced by a 22.3 million dollar middle-income housing project.

Roy Campanella was the guest of honor. Campy was at the last game at Ebbets Field in 1957 and was paralyzed in an automobile accident that off season. He was presented with his old 39 jersey and his locker. Another old catcher attending was 70 year old Otto Miller who caught the first game at Ebbets Field in 1913. Turning to a friend with tears in his eyes Miller said, "A lot of guys are afraid to cry. Not me, I'm not ashamed." Other former Brooklyn Dodgers on hand were Ralph Branca, Tommy Holmes and Carl Erskine who tossed two no-hitters while pitching at Ebbets Field. A regimental band played Auld Lang Syne and Lucy Moore sang The Star Spangled Banner. Campanella, now confined to a wheelchair, had some dirt scooped up around home plate to take home. Lee Allen, a historian from the Baseball Hall of Fame, received the key to the park and home plate to take back to Cooperstown, N.Y. Erskine posed for a photo with the wrecking ball, which was painted to resemble a baseball with red stitches, before it came crashing down on the visitor's dugout. While Ebbets Field was being torn down, the Polo Grounds was rumored to be going to the dogs. A racetrack owner from Phoenix, Arizona wanted to convert the stadium into a $15 million dog-racing track. Eventually, it would host the New York Mets for it's first two seasons while their new stadium was being constructed in Queens (on the proposed site where Robert Moses wanted to place the Dodgers years before).

Brooklyn faced more difficult times as it lost its shipyard jobs and the city as a whole went through turbulent decades of population shift and increased crime problems. As a new century has unfolded, the borough has undergone a renaissance. Housing prices are rising and many areas are now quite affluent. Down by Nathan's in Coney Island there is a new minor league Class A ballpark of the New York Mets, KeySpan Park. The team is called the Cyclones, named after the Coney Island roller coaster that is visible over the outfield stands. Every game is a sellout even though baseball isn't as popular as it used to be, Baseball has started to try and heal the wounds and the park is a source of civic pride. Mets owner Fred Wilpon is a Brooklyn native and played at Lafayette High where Sandy Koufax began his rise to stardom.

The Brooklyn Dodger Hall of Fame, after being located for some time at a middle school by the old Ebbets Field location, is now installed at the KeySpan Park. Marty Adler, a retired Brooklyn teacher, got the idea off the ground. "I was at my school (Jackie Robinson Junior High) which in 1977 was going to celebrate it's 10th anniversary. We decided to not only celebrate the school's anniversary but Jackie's 30th entry into baseball," Adler said. "So when we put it together, we got people from all places and started asking around for different things. That was the germ that started it and it took off from there," he said. "The school was actually on the parking lot side of third base to left field side (of Ebbets Field).

There is a plaque now at Sullivan and McKeever Place that mentions Ebbets Field where the apartment complex still stands. A sign nearby says NO BALL PLAYING ALLOWED. It's ironic since some of the finest major league baseball ever witnessed was played there. Like a long lost sweetheart, Ebbets Field conjures up blissful memories and a painful ache in the heart plus a lump in the throat of many who spent part of their lives there.

Ebbets Field brings back memories of baseball when it was seen as a sport and not a business. It also was a time when players were seen as friends and one "of us" instead as aloof millionaires. Too many people still see it as a special place, in a special time for that memory to be false. Ebbets Field still holds a place that's unique in baseball history.

It was Brooklyn's Baseball Shrine.

About the Author

Joseph McCauley has many books on historic ball parks but noted that none focused on one of the most famous ball parks of all, Brooklyn's Ebbets Field. A trip to the Baseball Hall of Fame in Cooperstown, New York motivated him to write a book on Ebbets Field in 2002.

Two years later, after interviews with fans and 11 Brooklyn Dodgers, trips to the Brooklyn Historical Society, Brooklyn Library and the Library of Congress, the book has been completed.

Joseph has a journalism degree from Wayne State. For the past 25 years, he has been a USPS letter carrier but never lost his love of writing.

Joseph has 3 children and resides with his wife in Northville, Michigan.